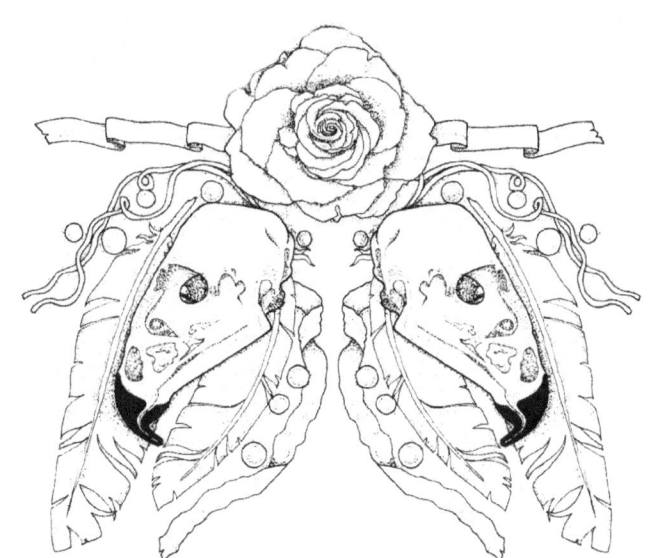

For Colors of Whimsy III, I would like to thank the Taiwan Team. They include Debbie Lai, Jenny Wei, Jovian Ke, Nancy43, Leaf Yeh, Lilan Chen, Jodi Ho and Rover Hsiao.
They have worked so hard to bring life to my illustrations and I can't thank them enough!

You guys rock my world!

The front cover is colored
by Jenny Wei
and
back cover is by Leaf Yeh
and Lilan Chen

Copyright 2015 Colors of Whimsy III
All rights reserved by Bev Choy. Duplication of pages for personal use are allowed.
You are invited to color the pages, then scan/post your colored versions to social networks, mentioning the book title and author/artist (Colors of Whimsy III).
All artwork and images are protected by copyright laws. This book or any portion thereof may not, otherwise, be reproduced and/or distributed or transmitted without the express written permission of the artist/publisher of Colors of Whimsy III.

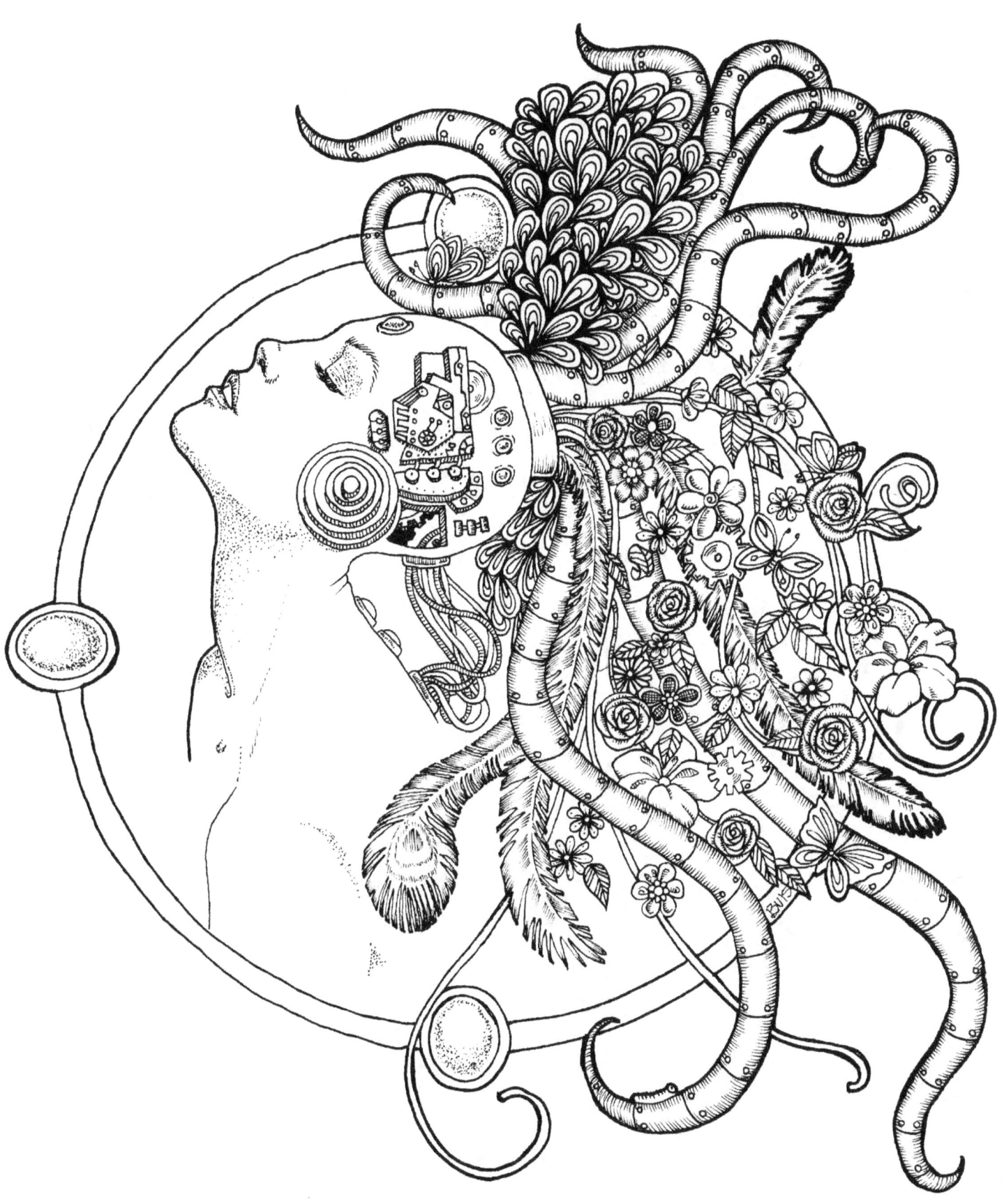

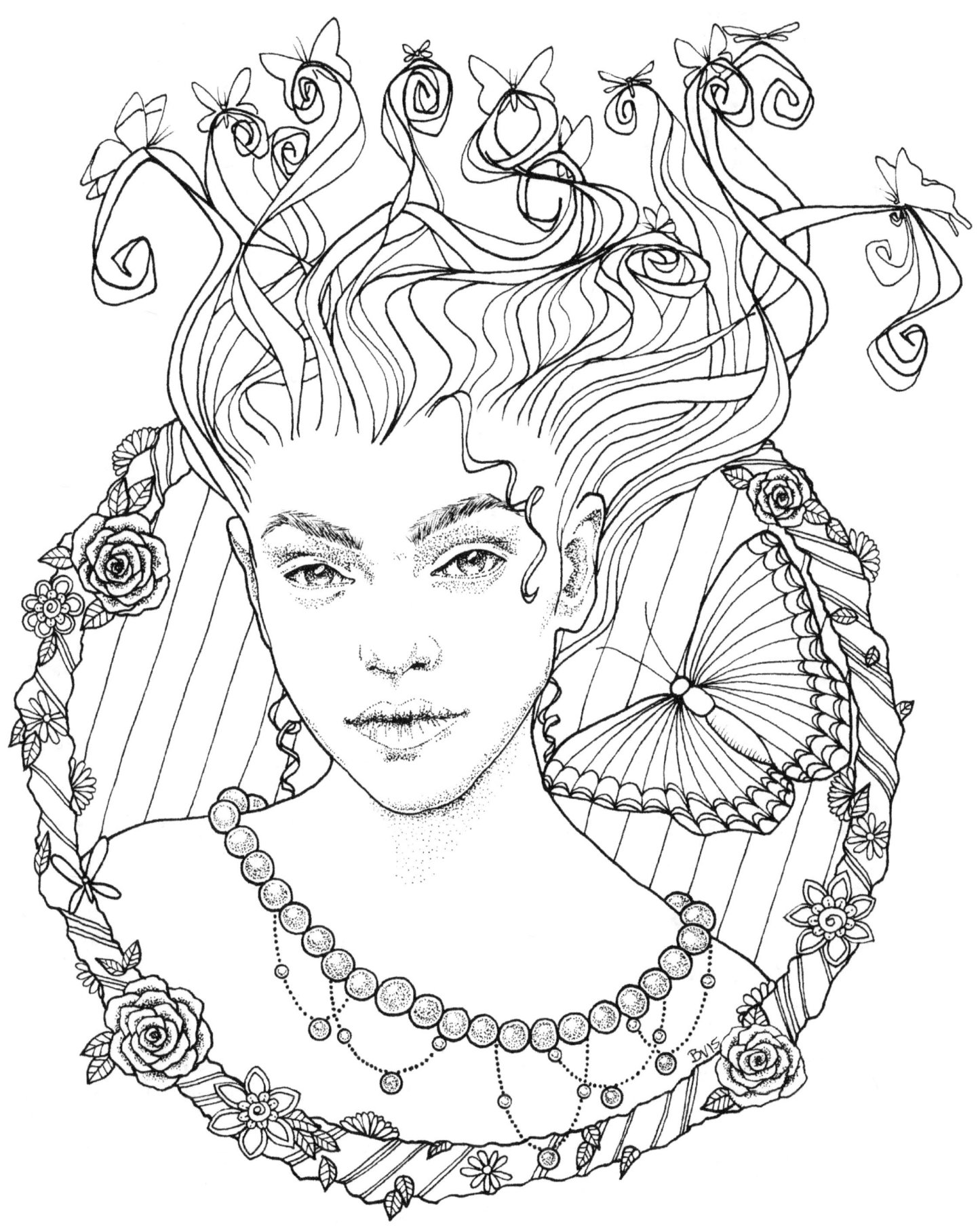

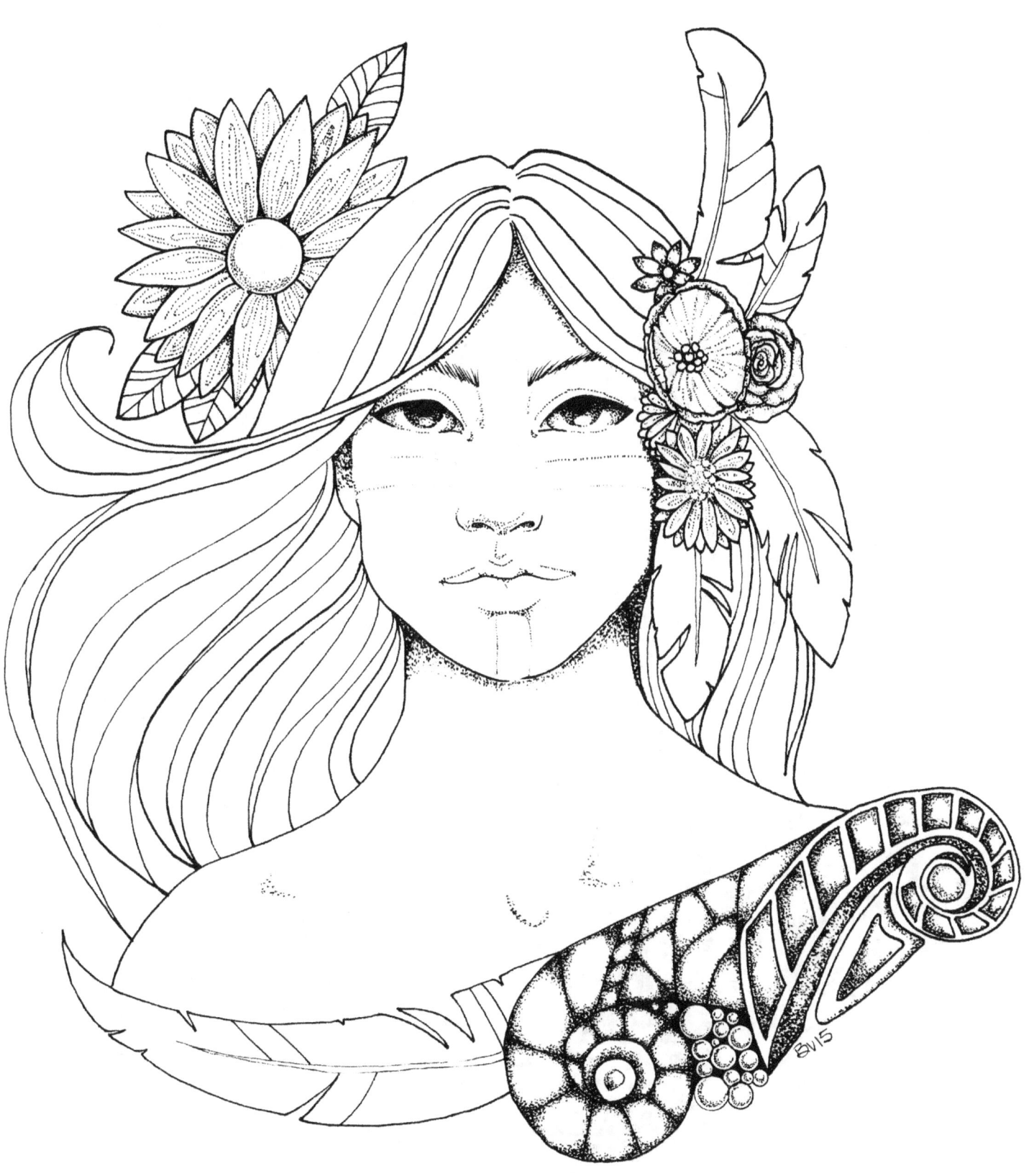

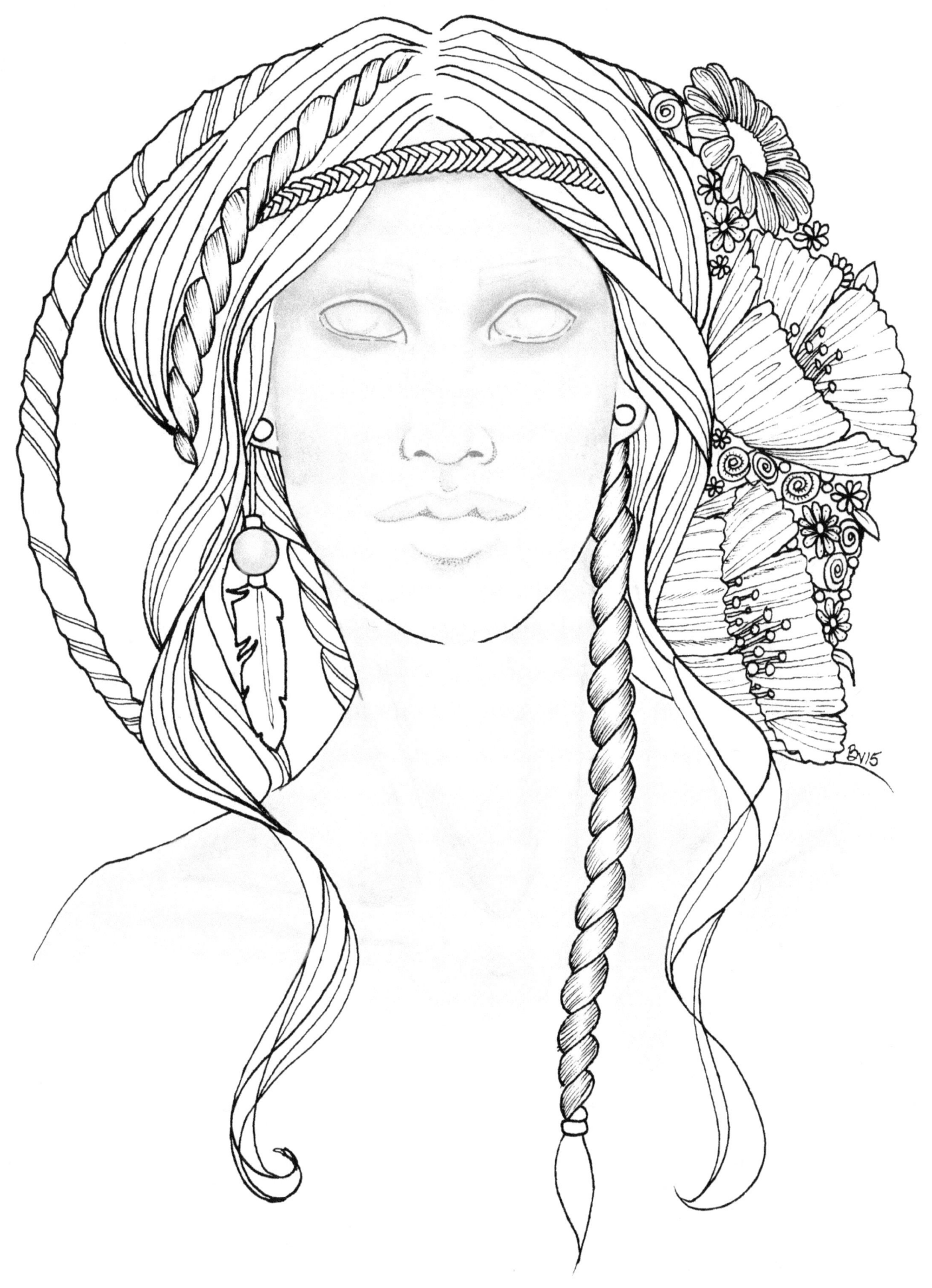

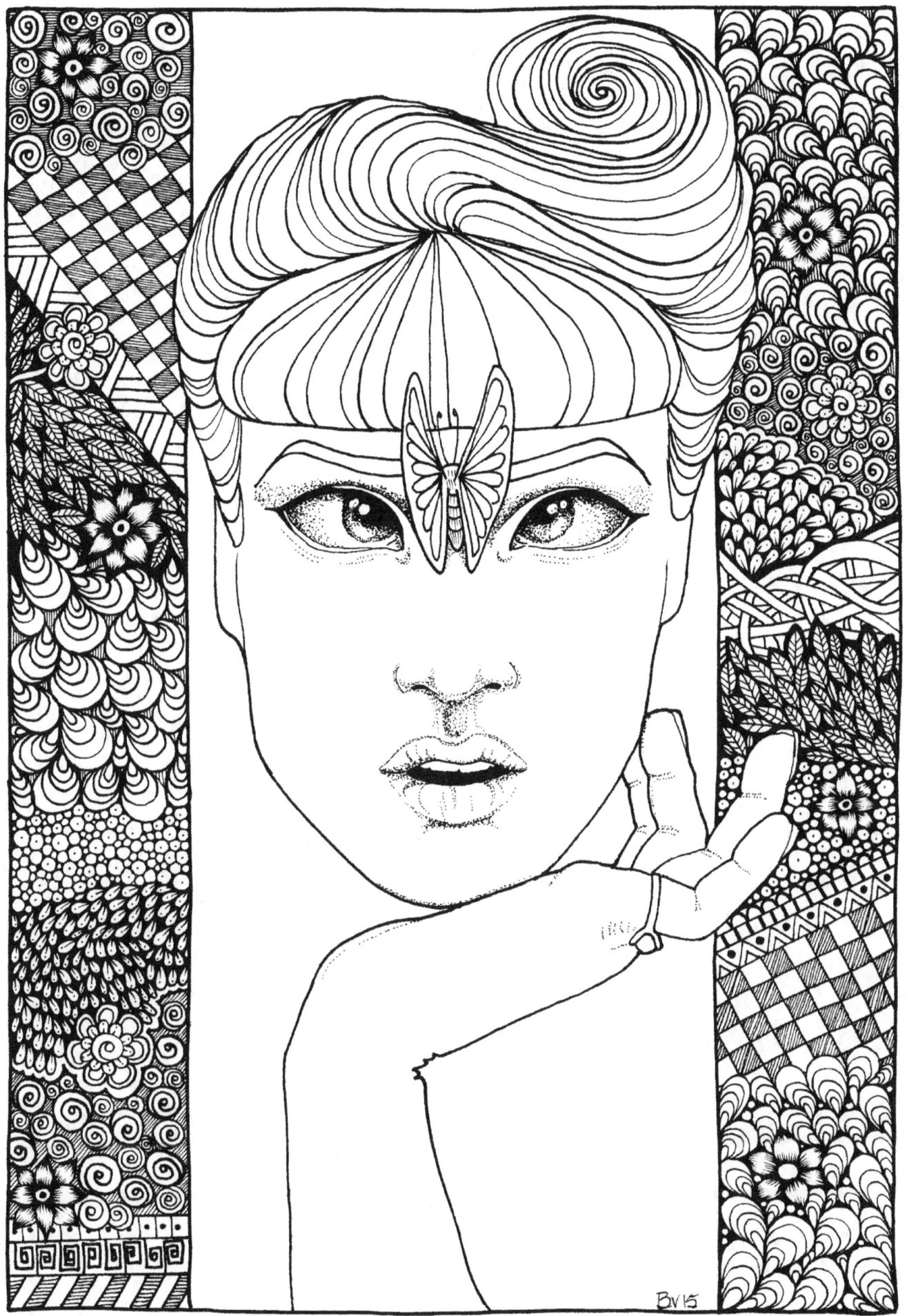

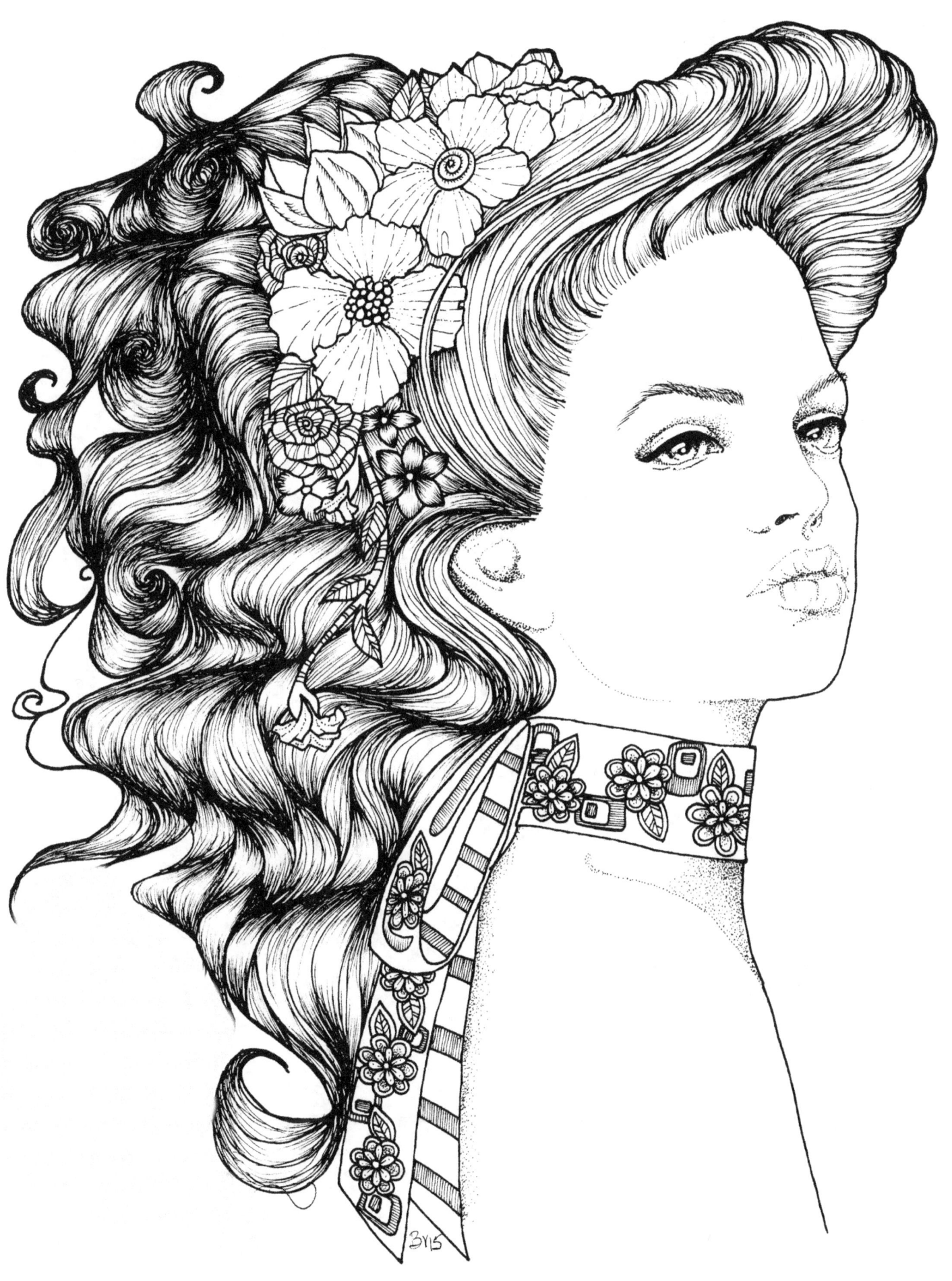

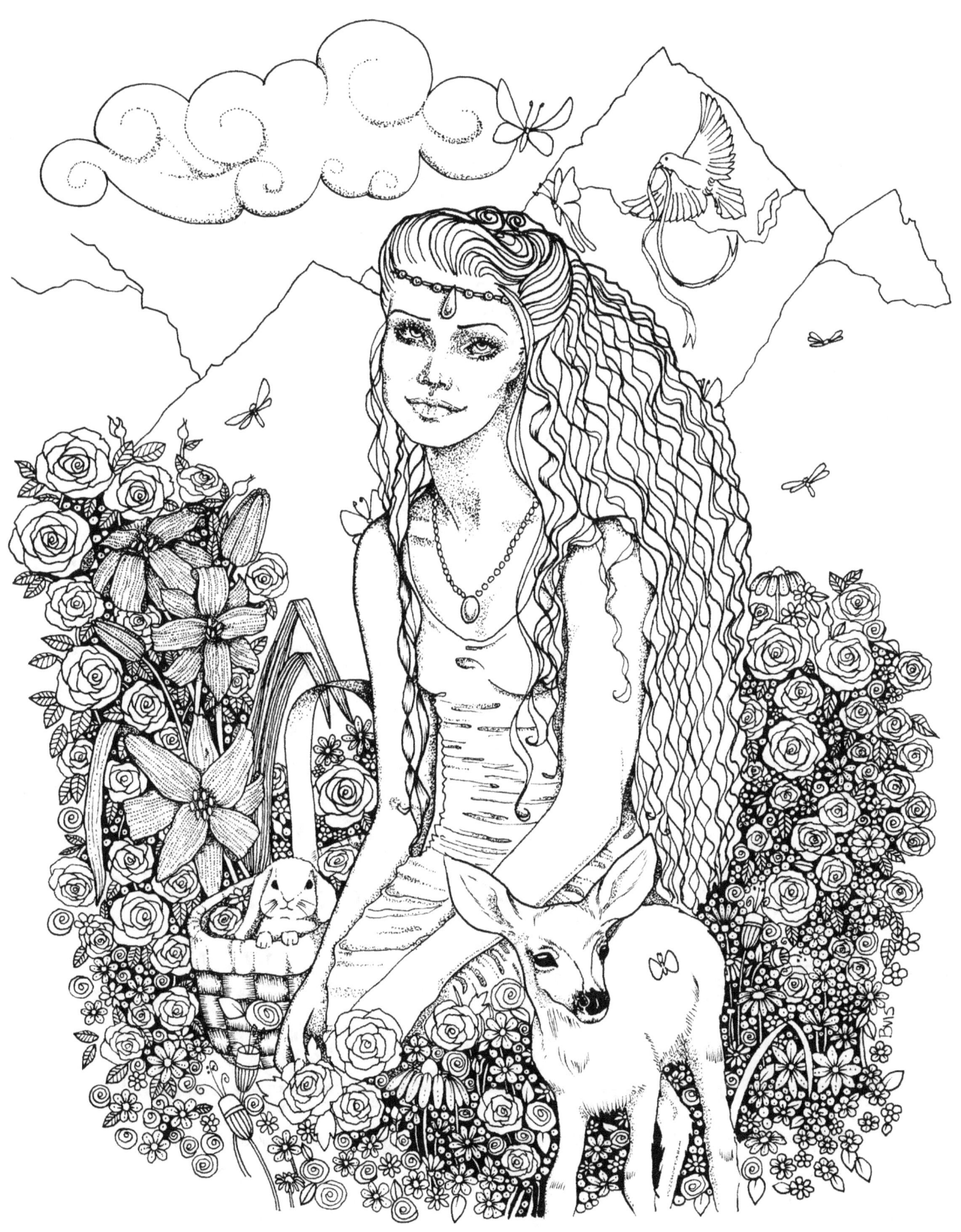

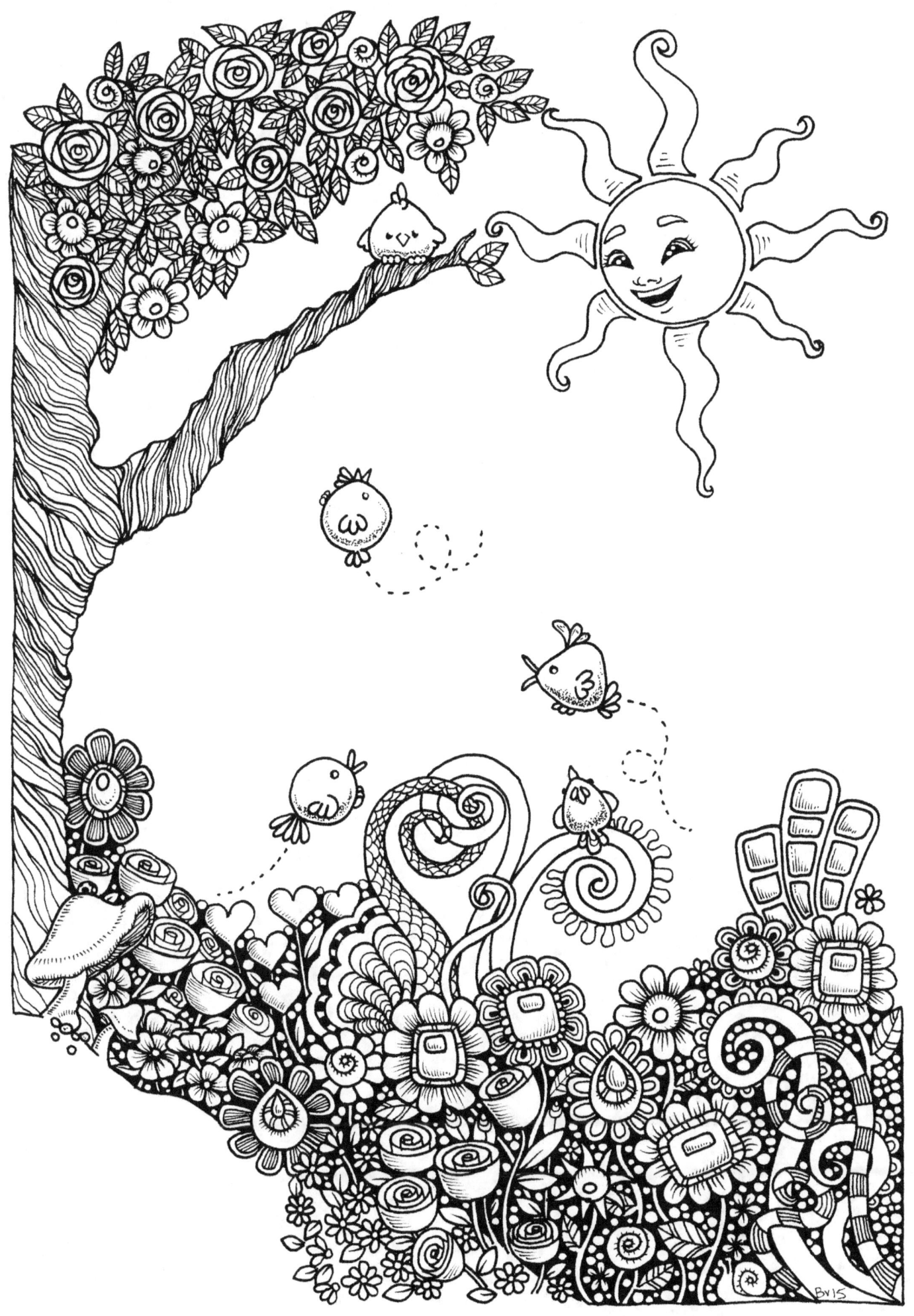

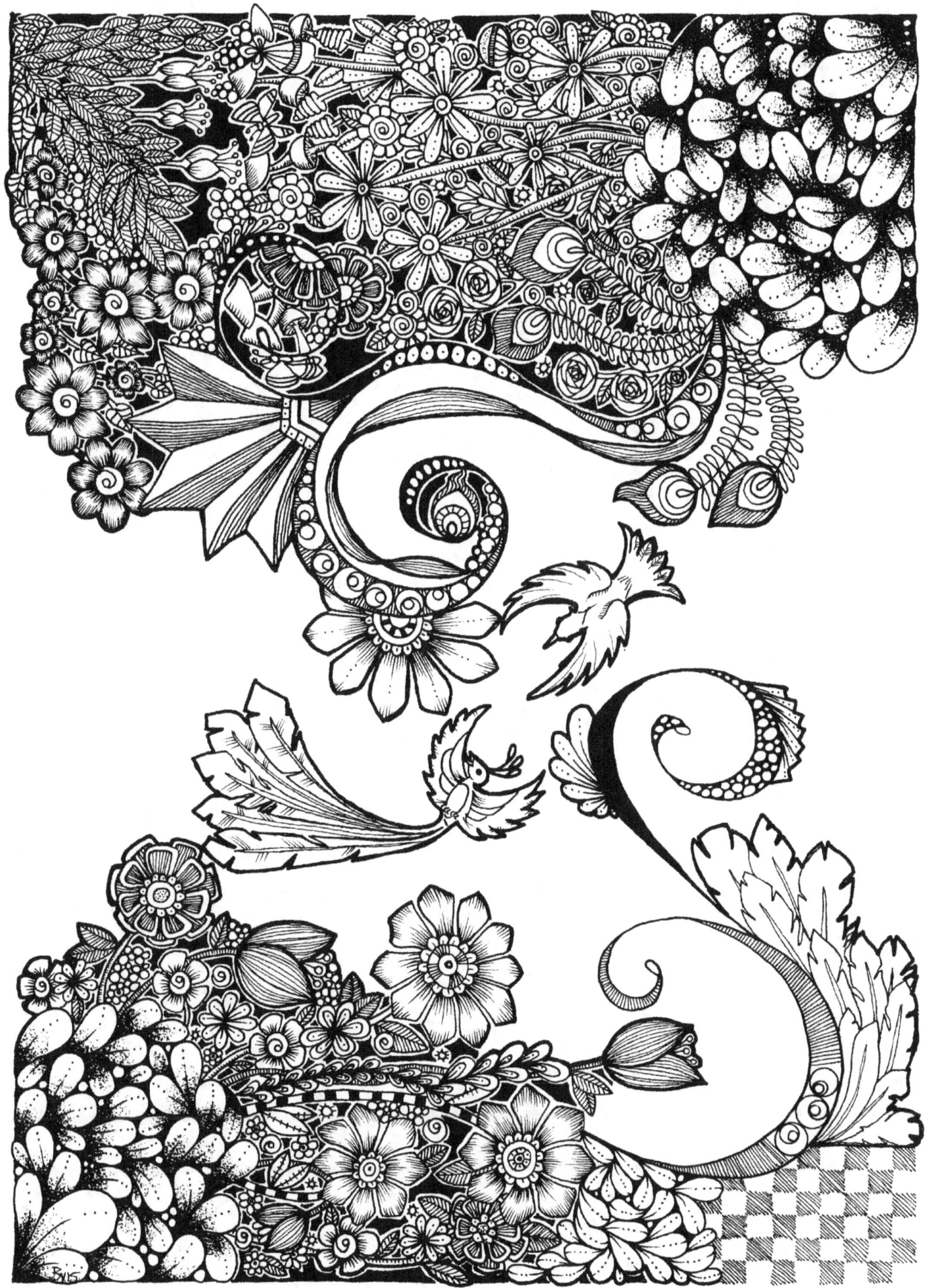

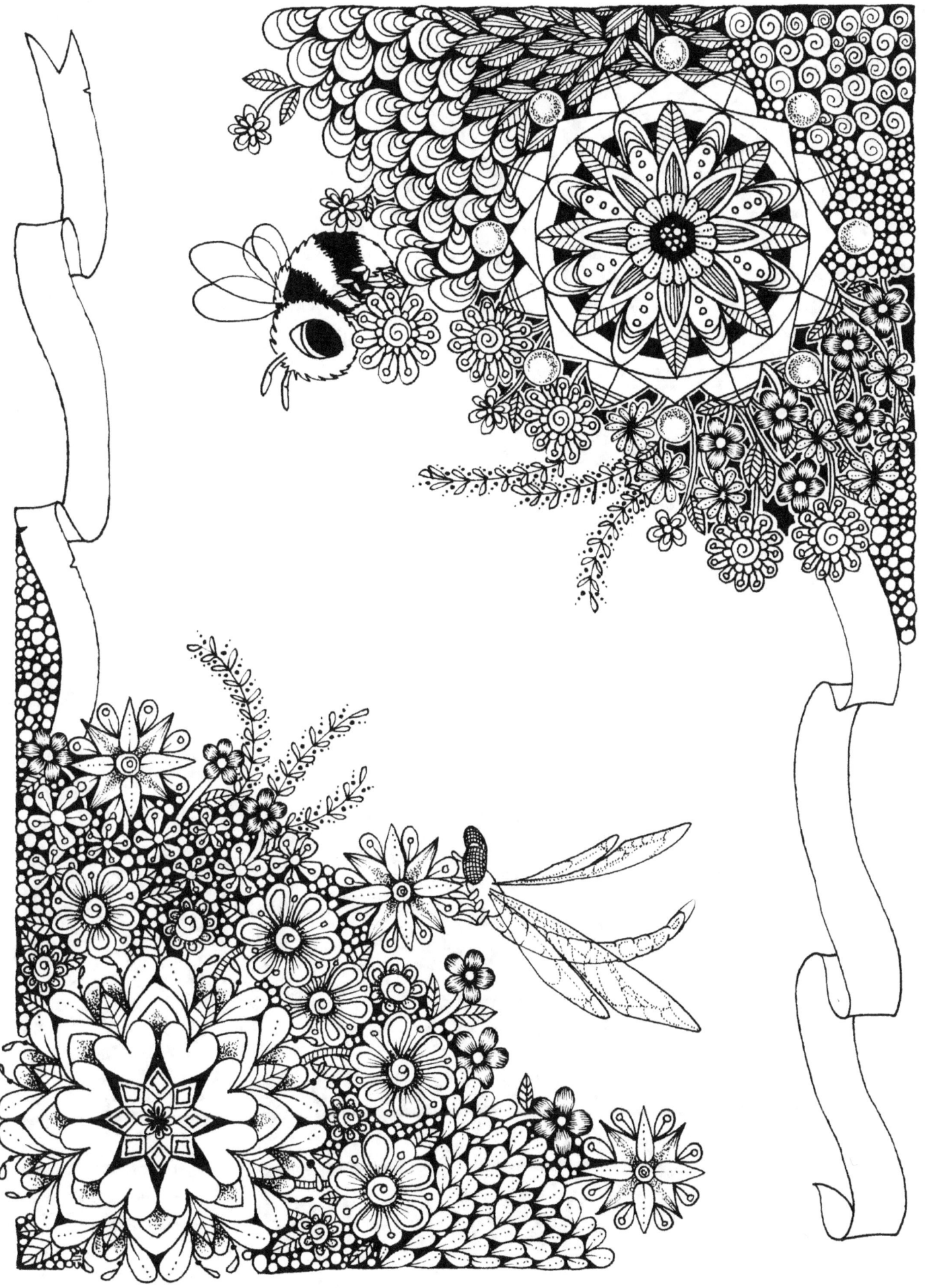

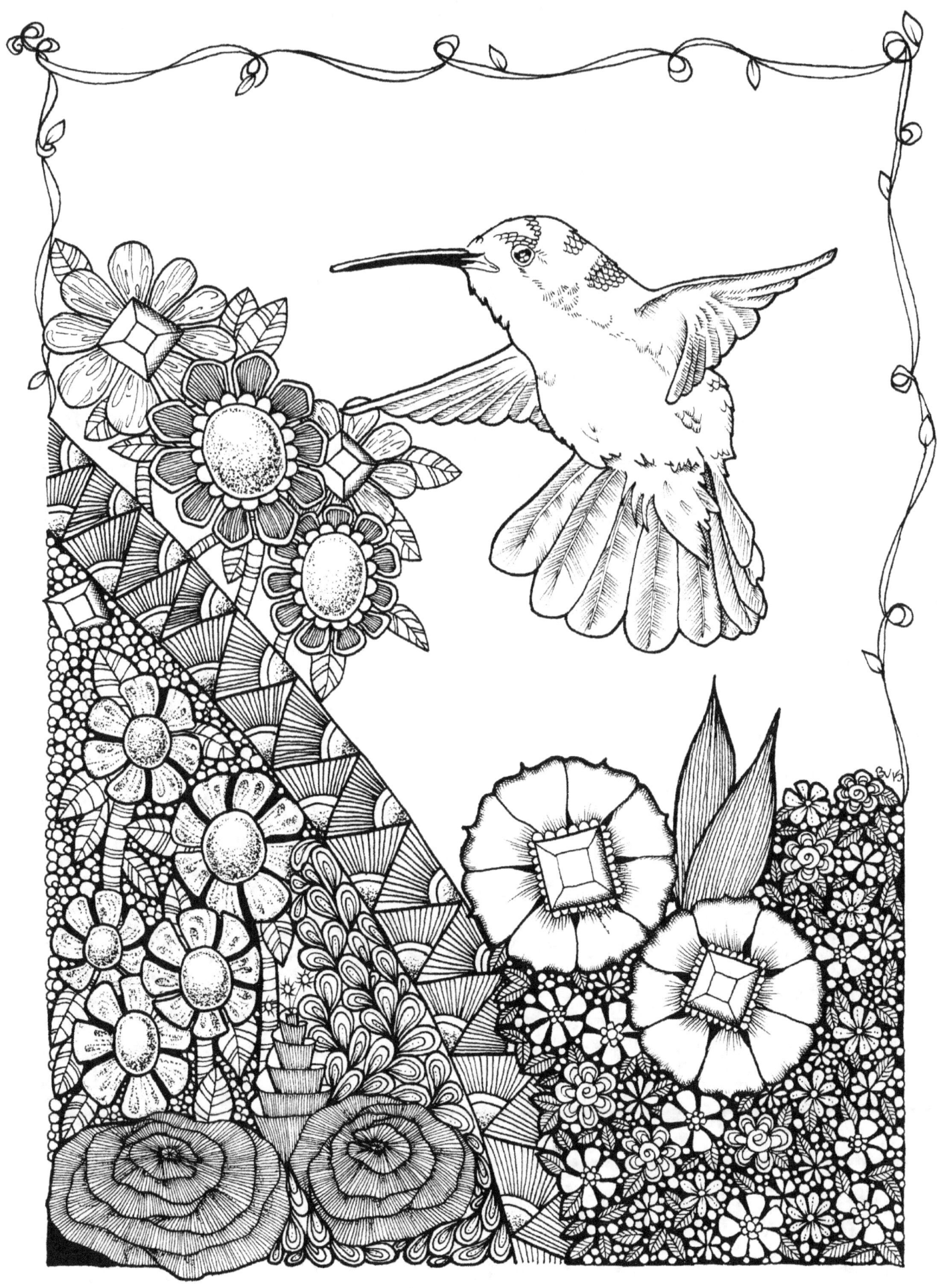

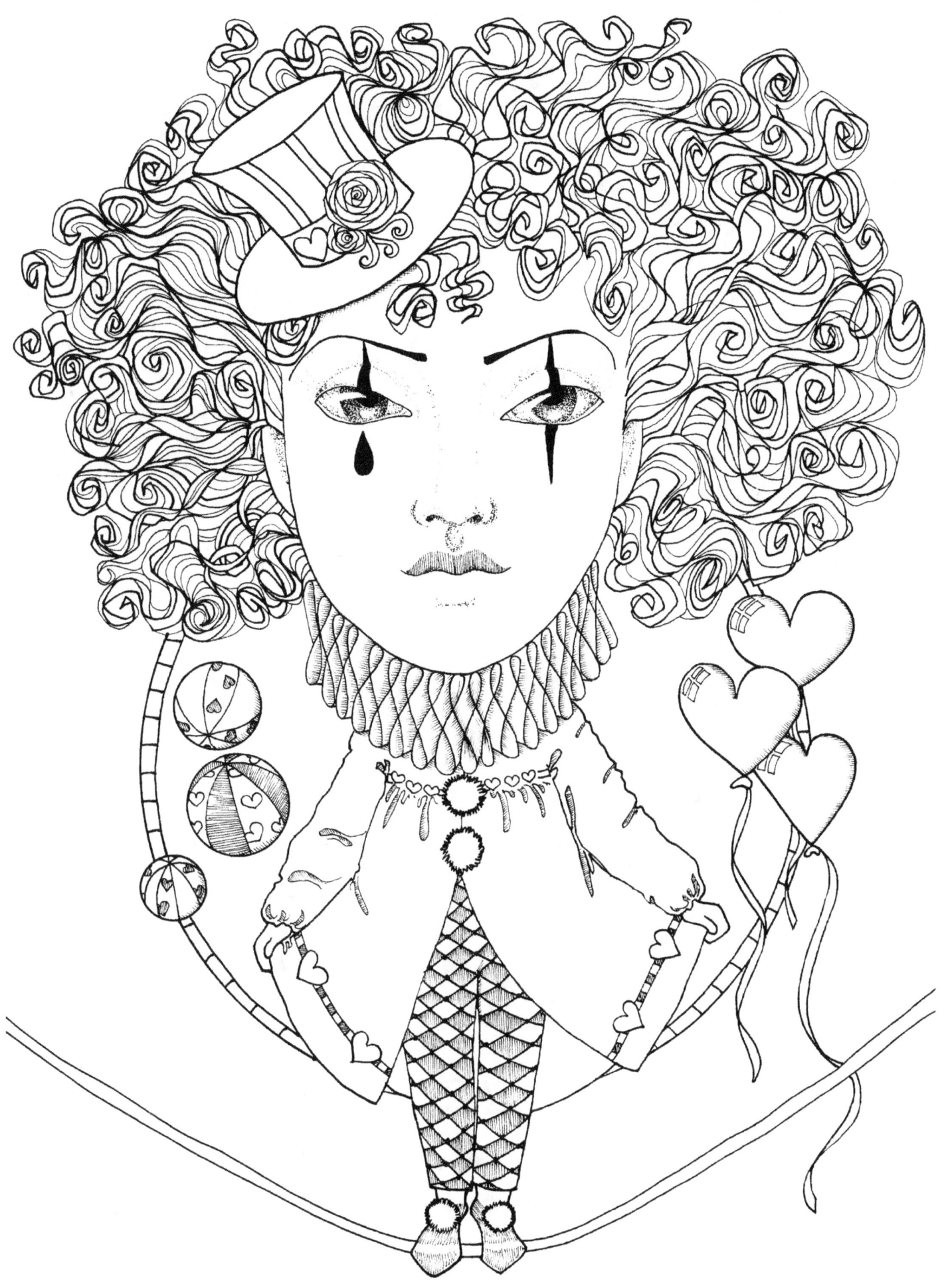

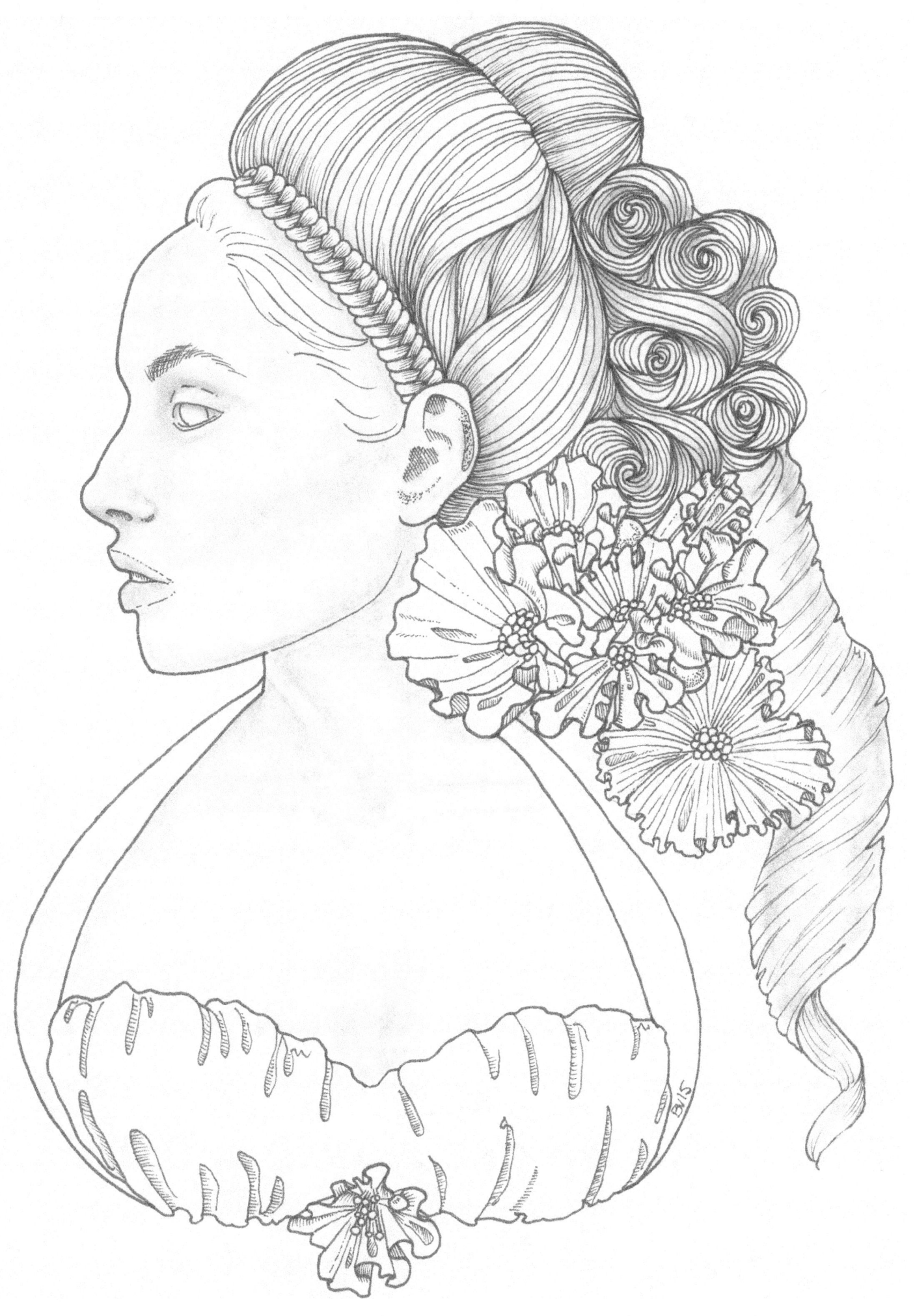

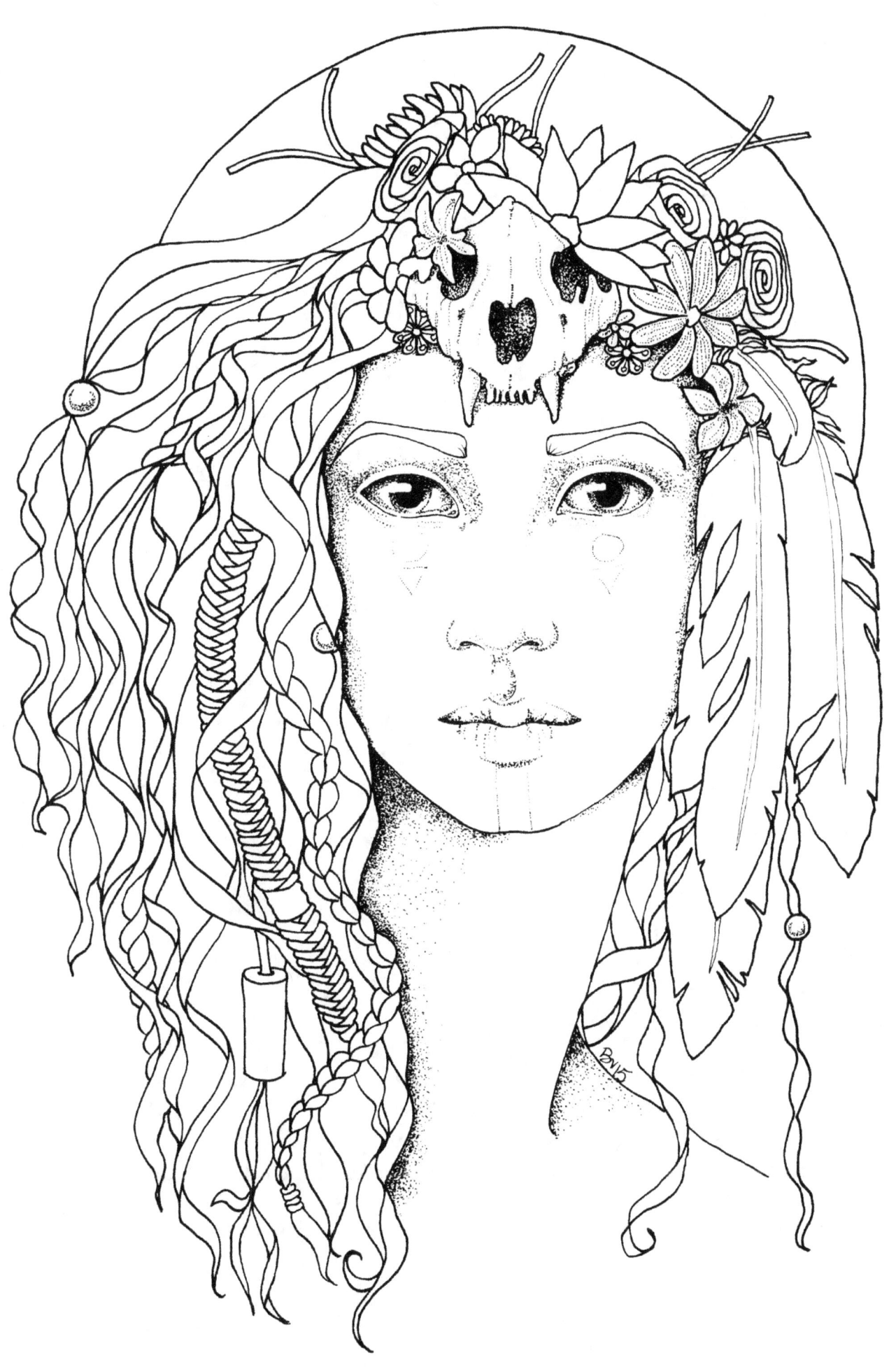

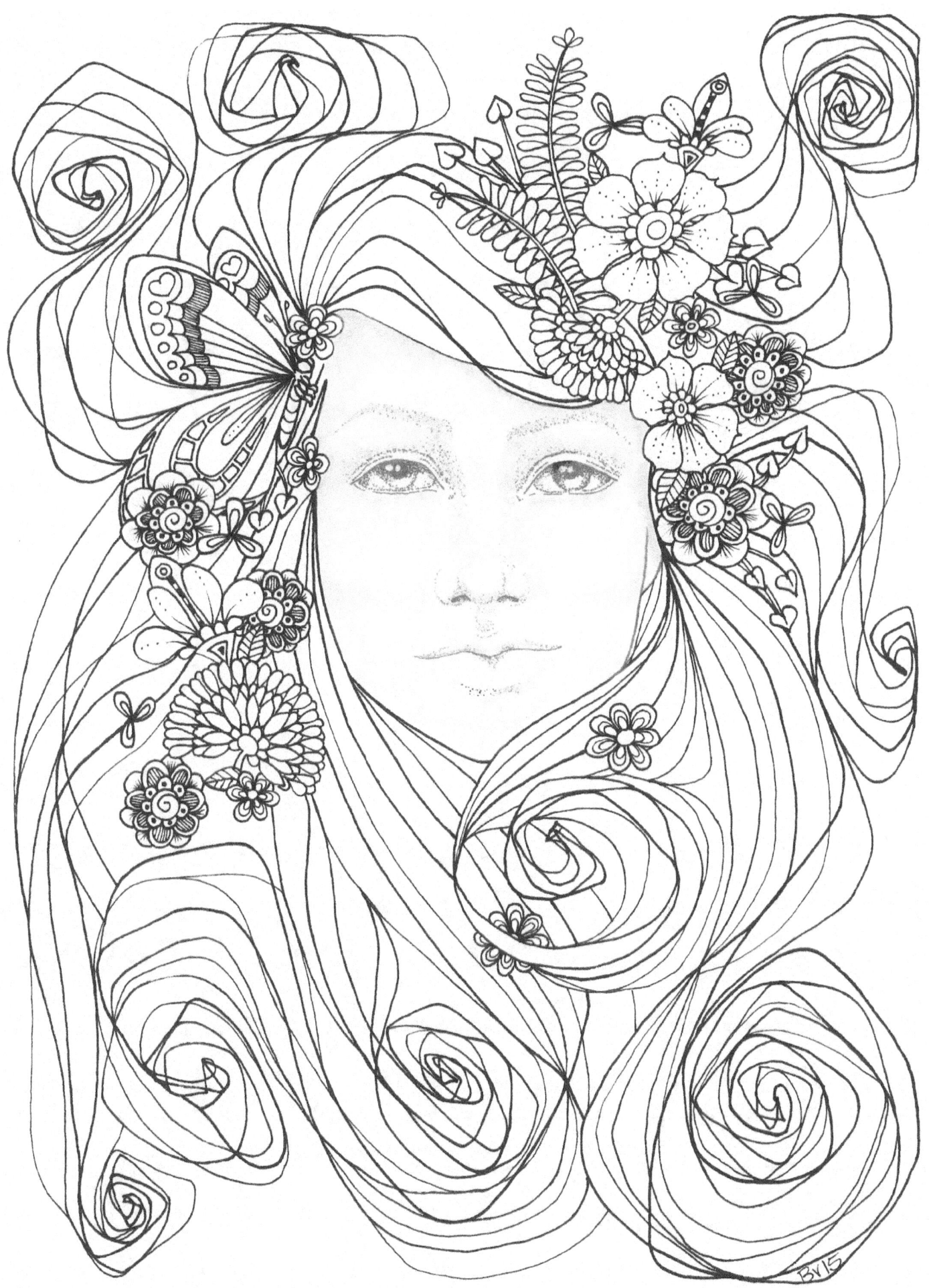

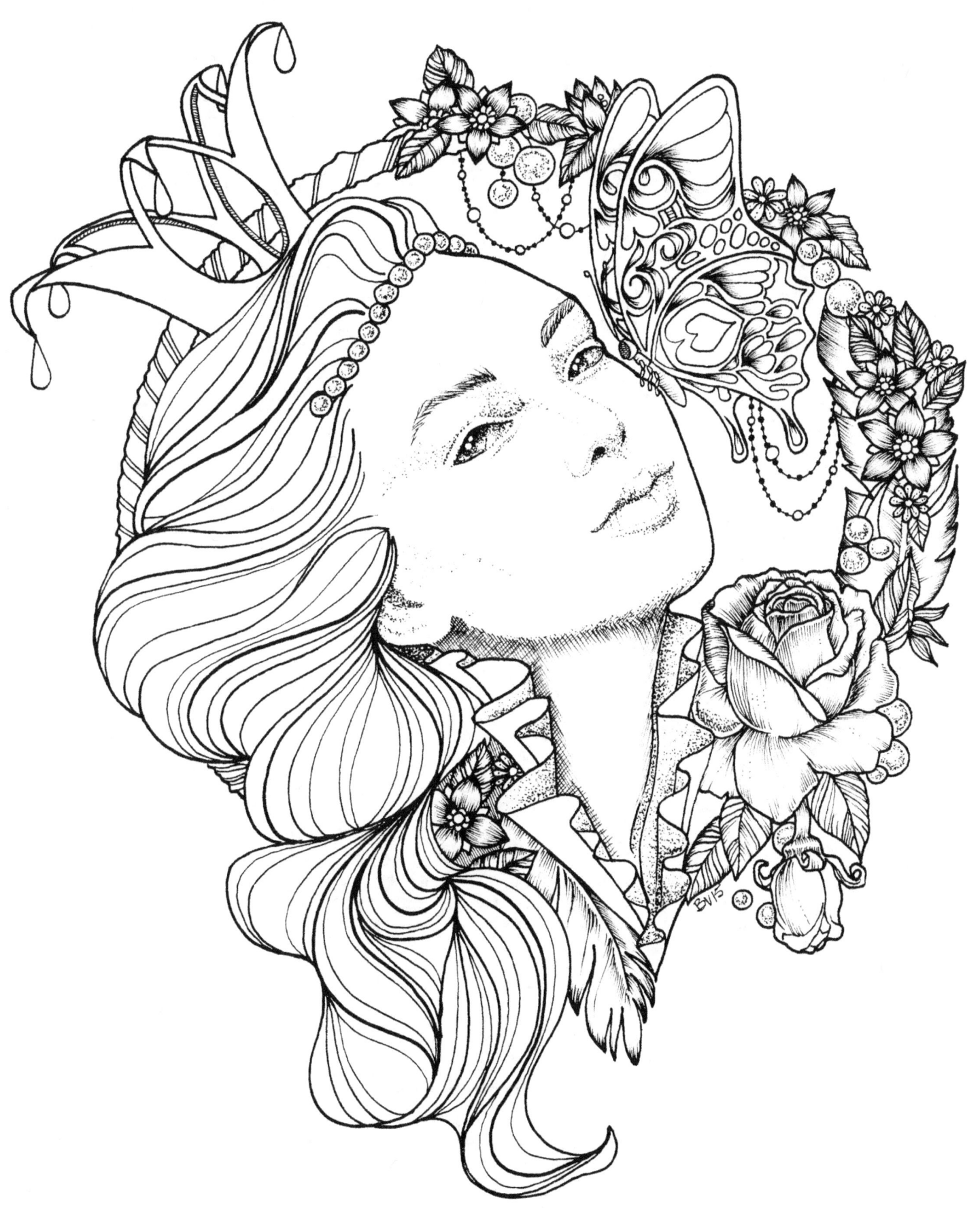

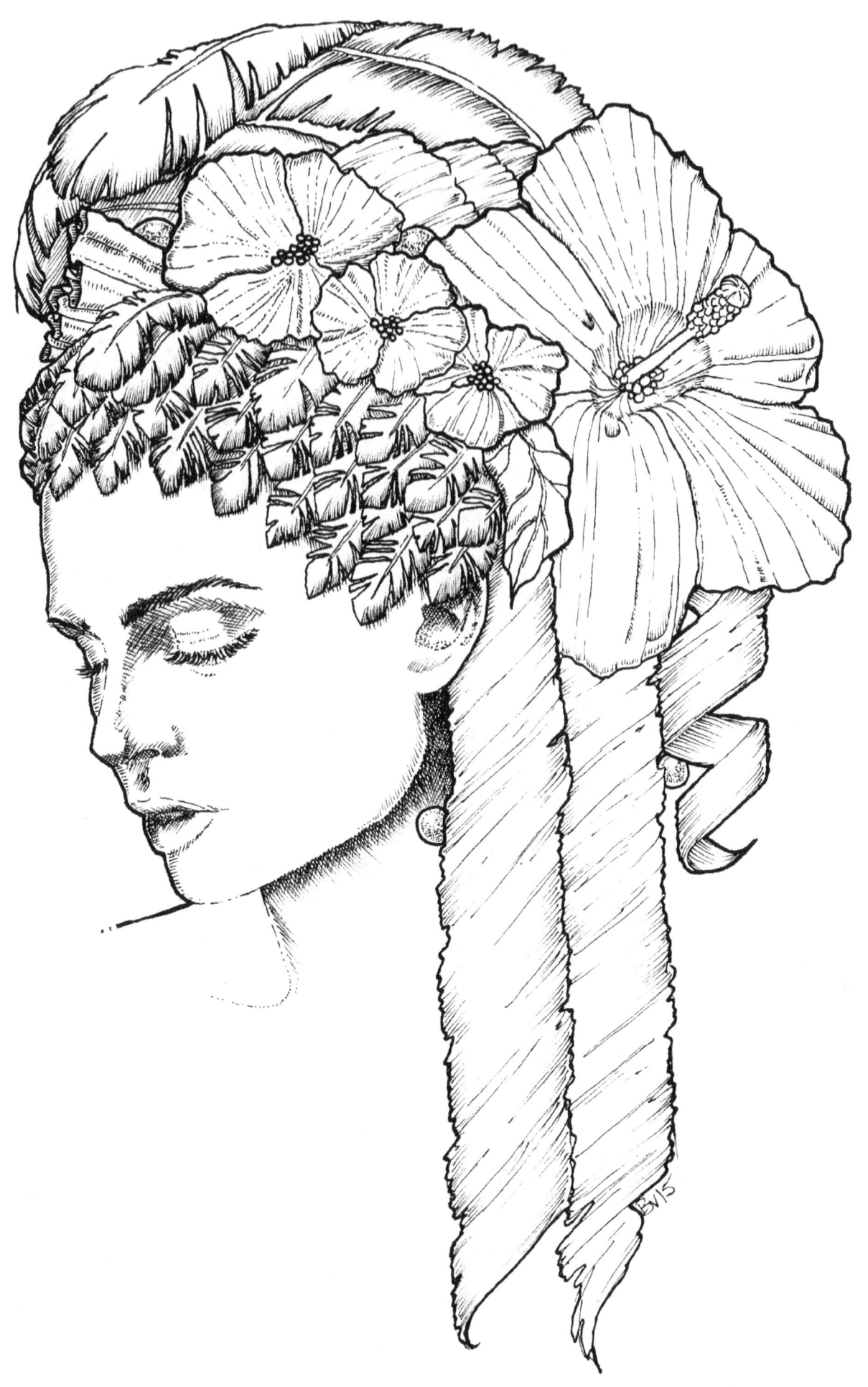

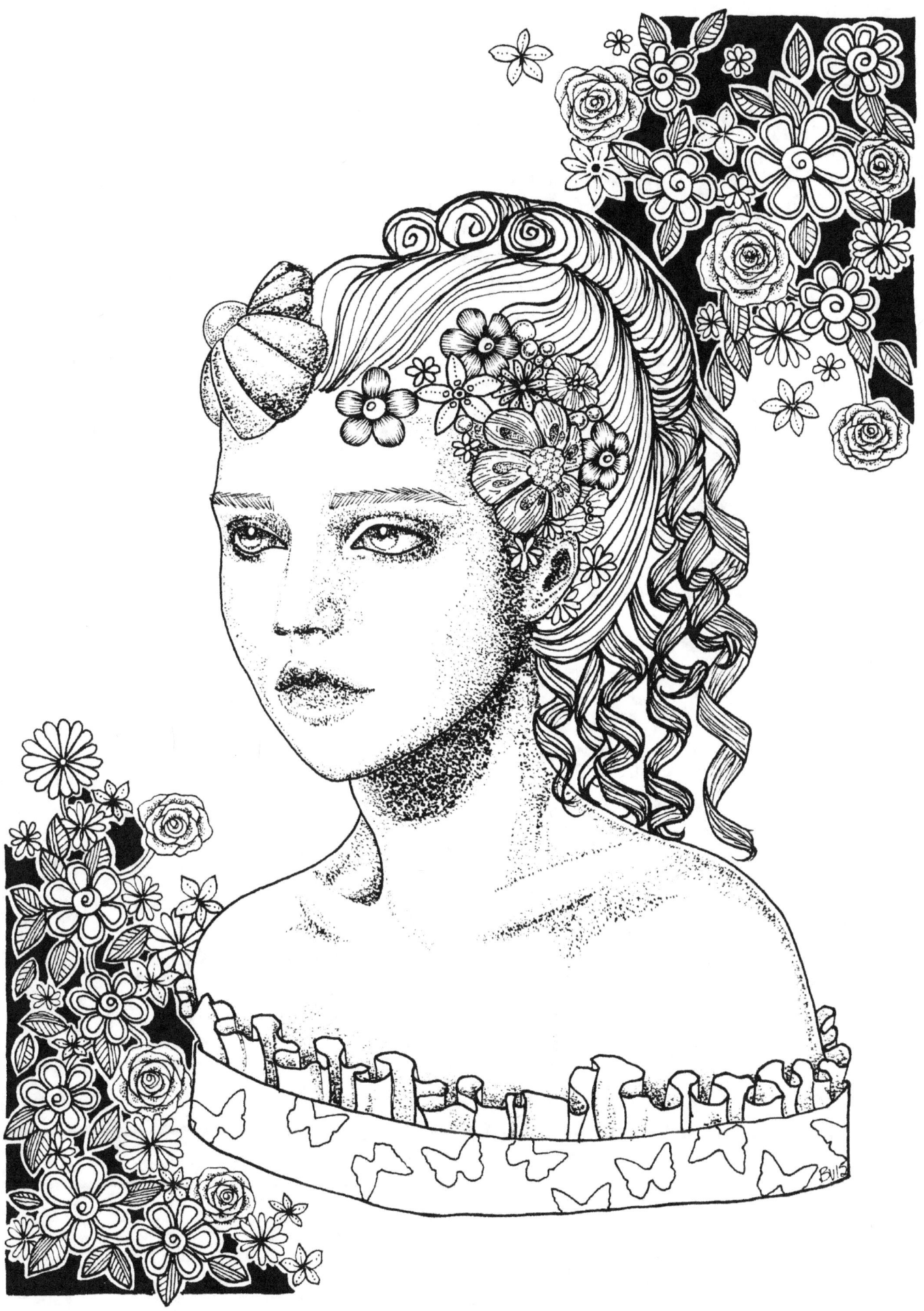

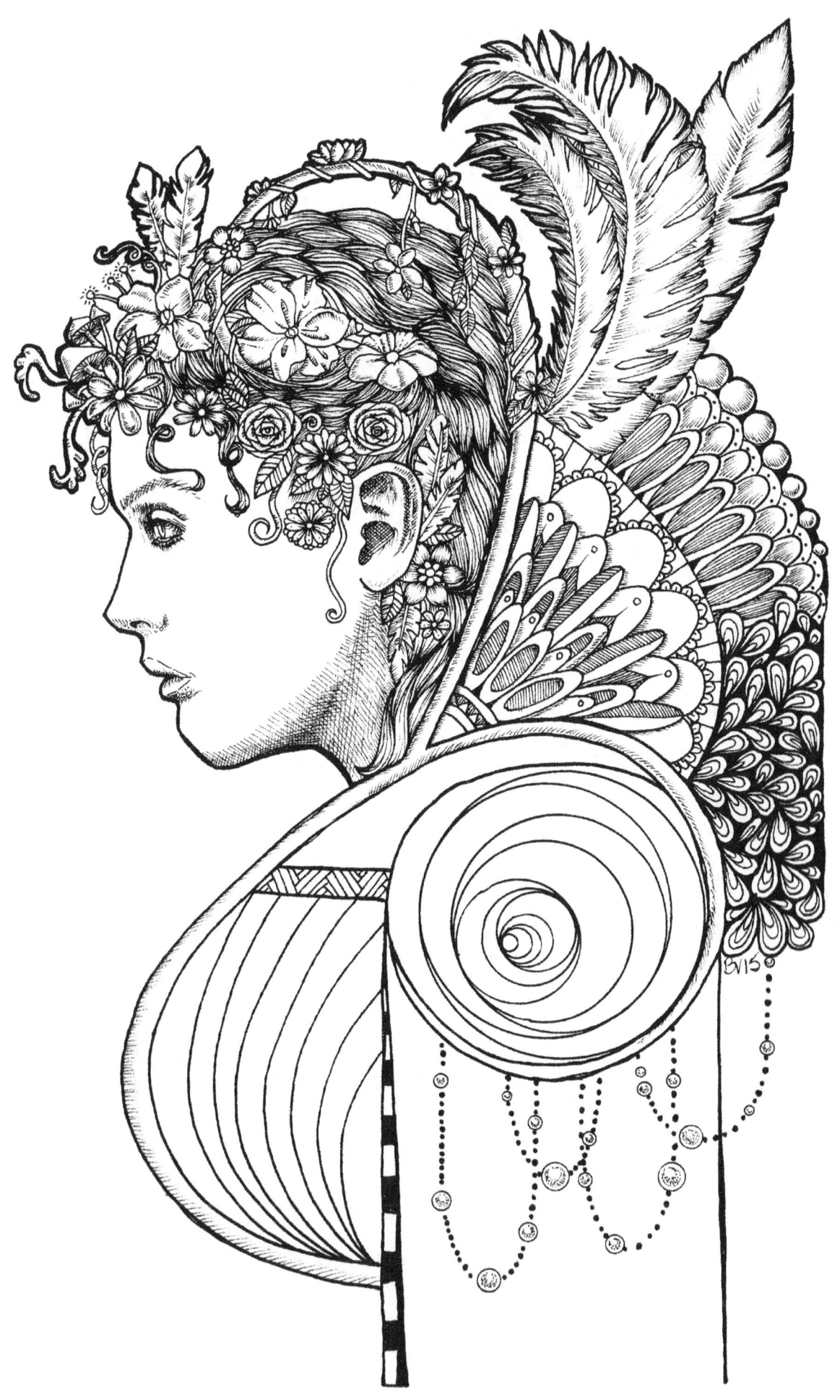

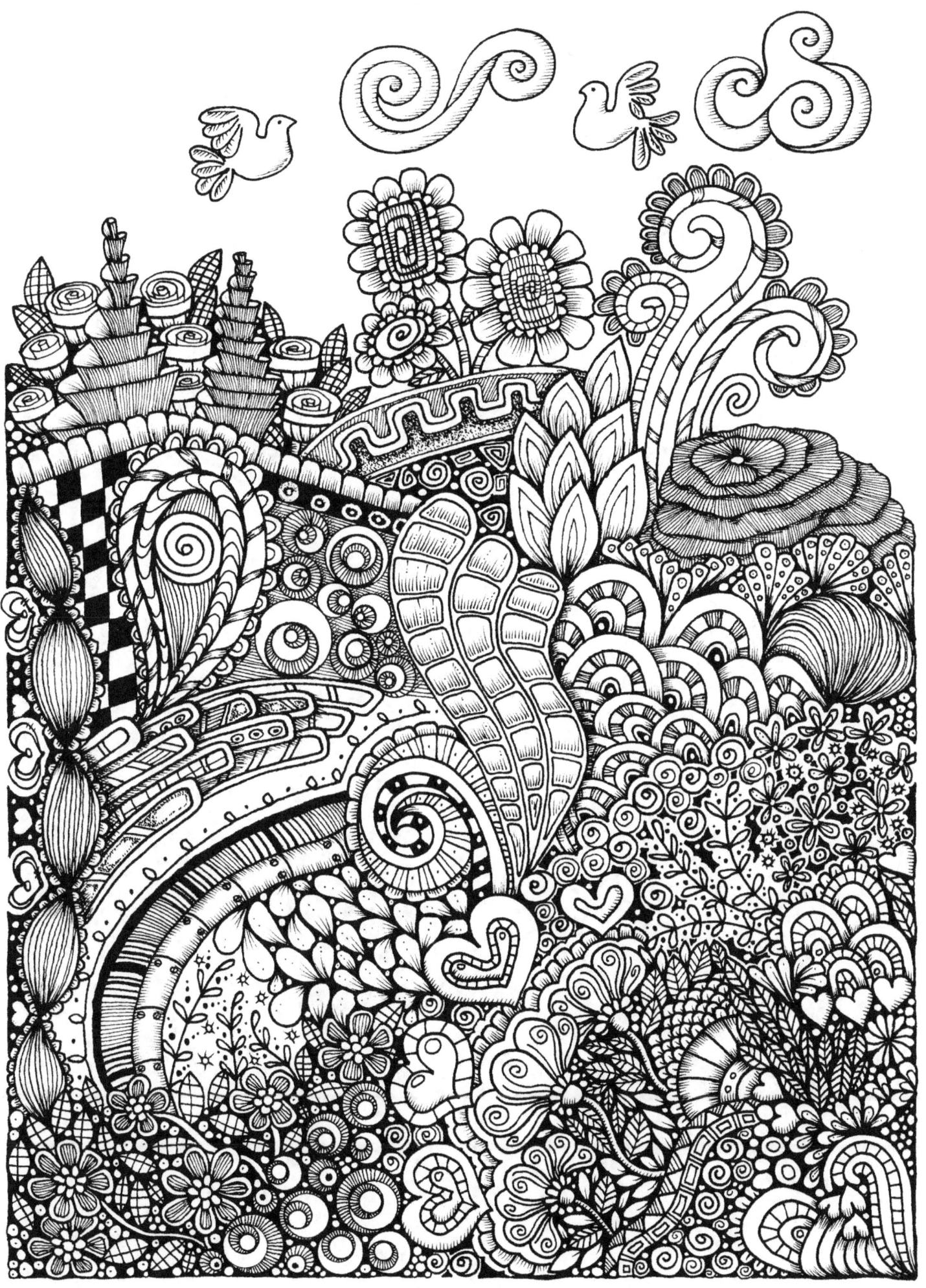

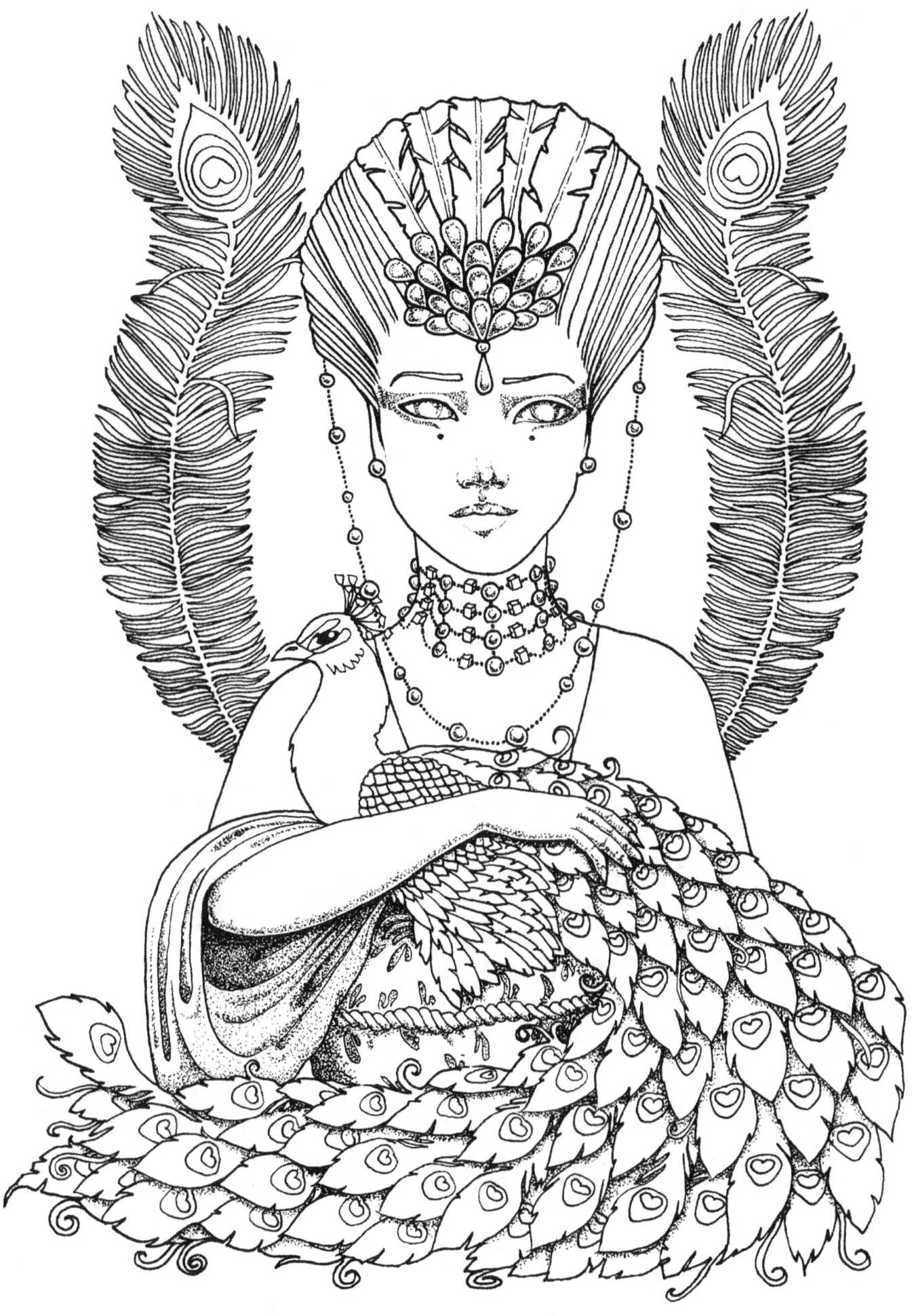

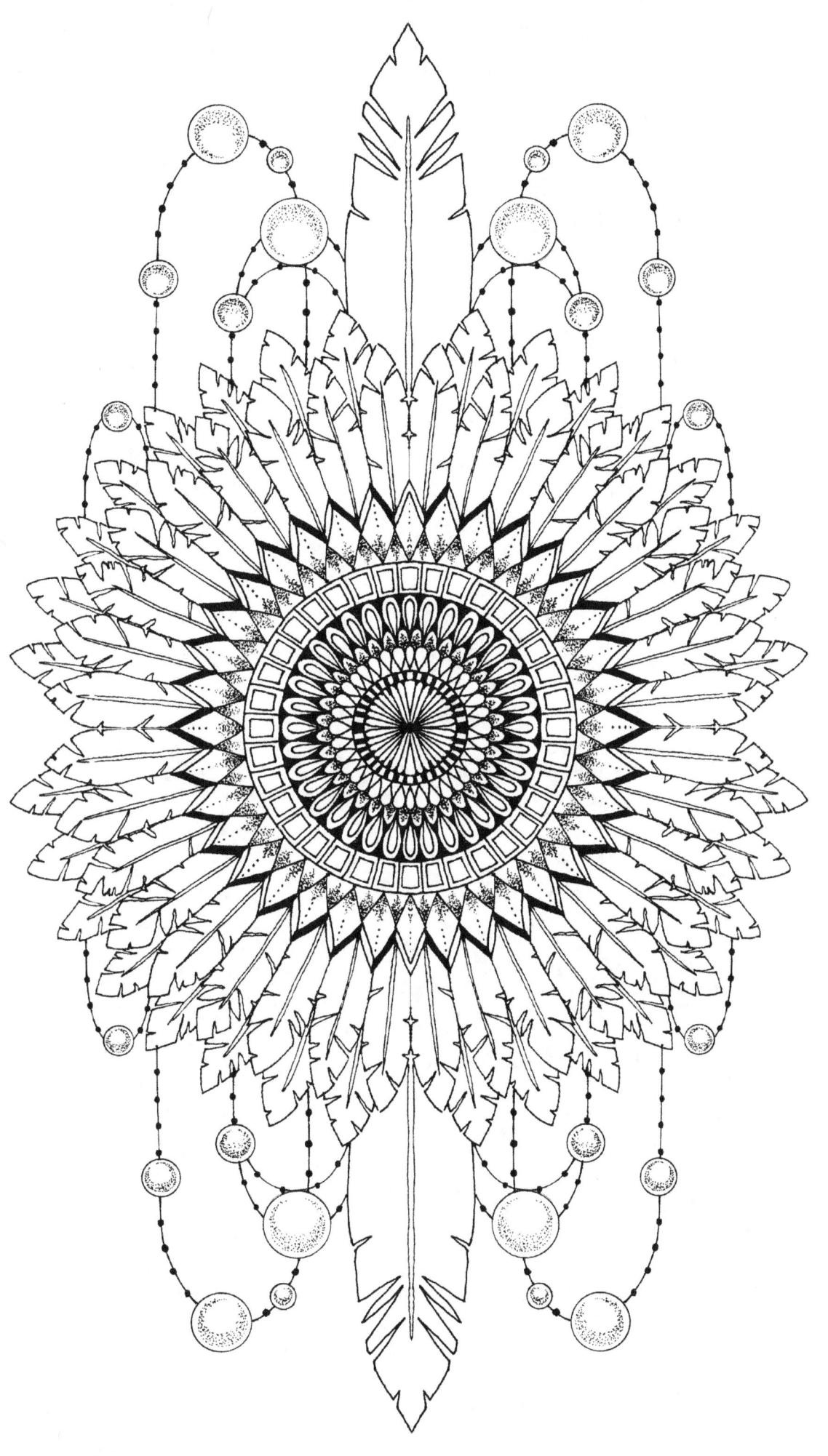

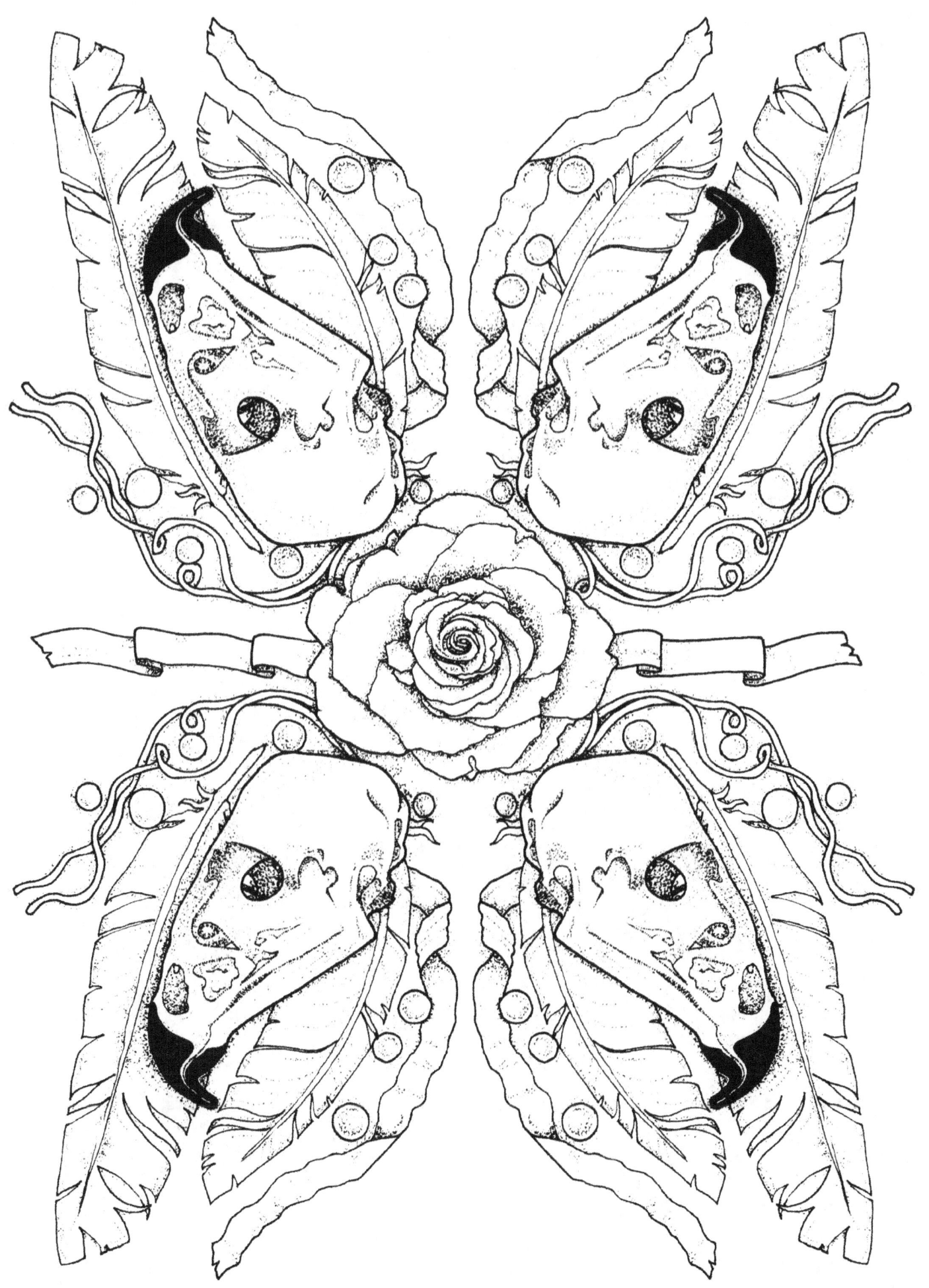

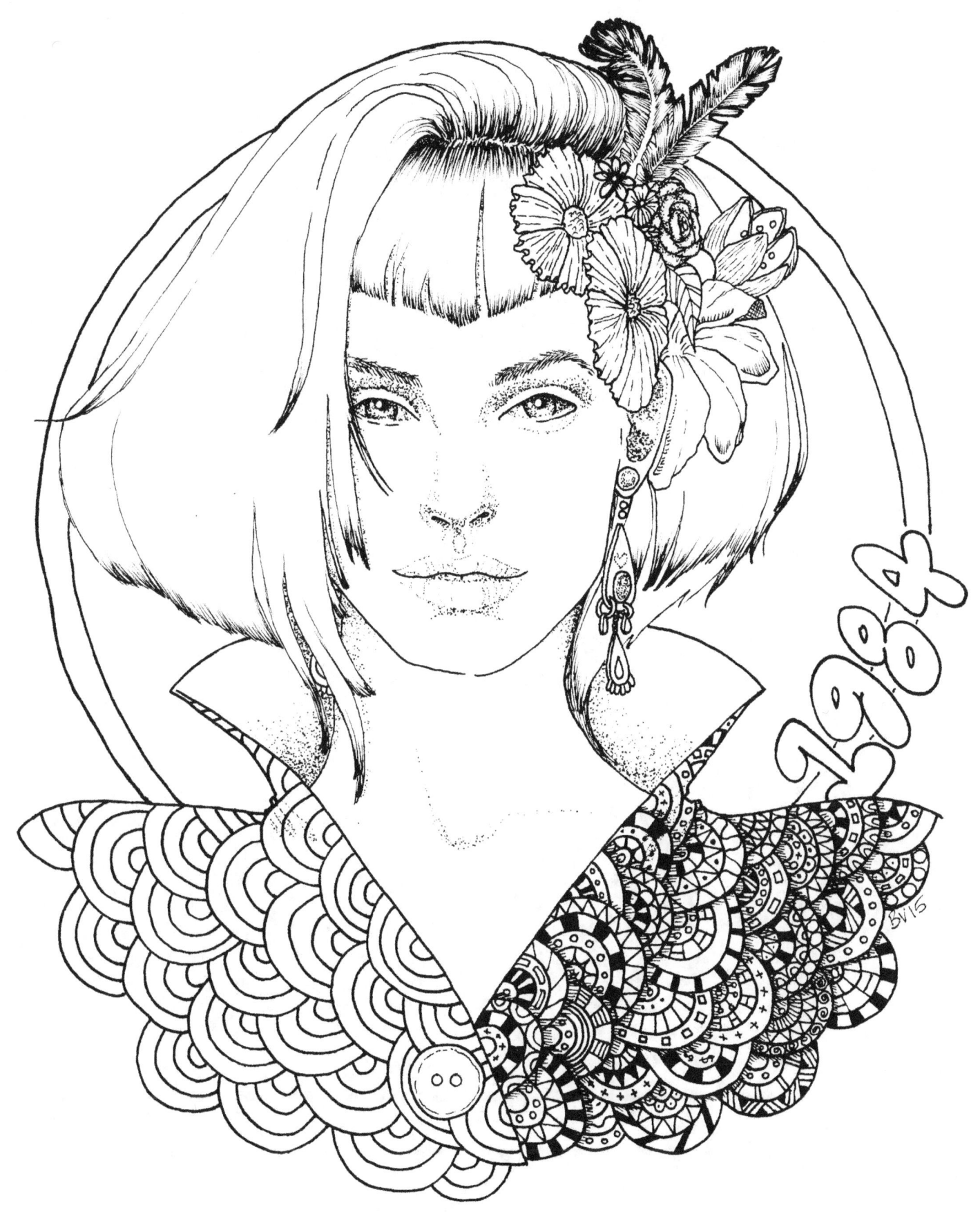

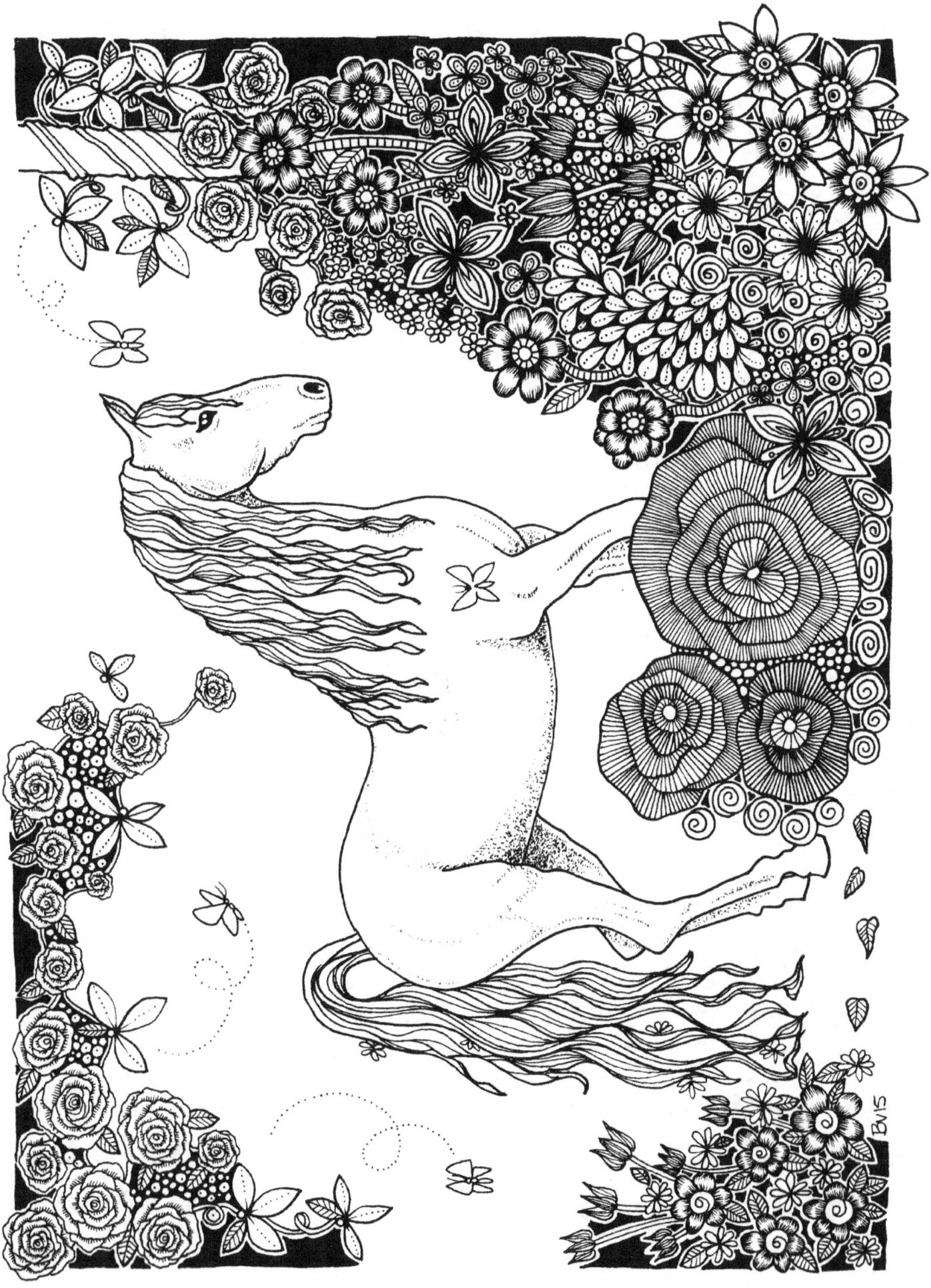

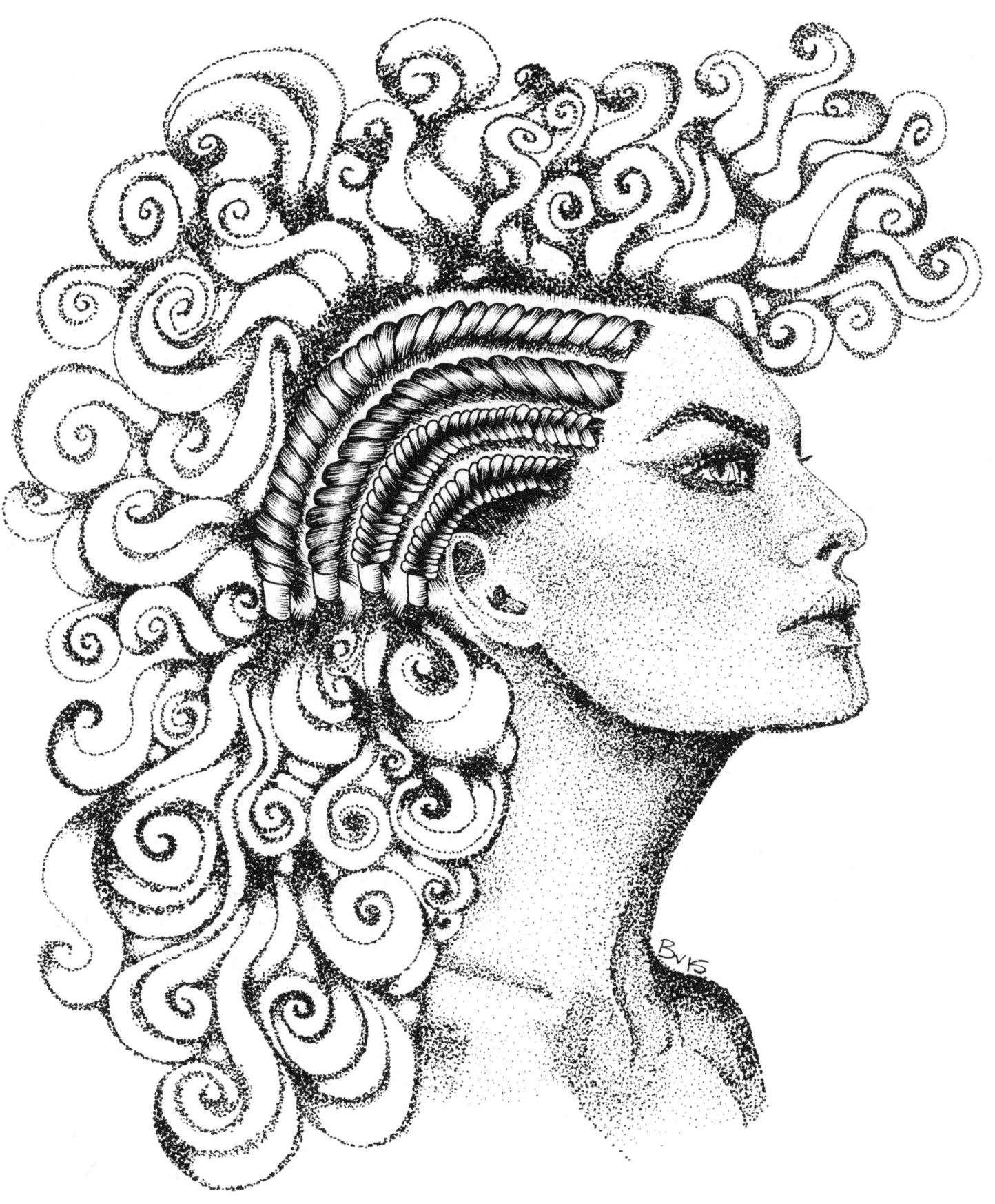

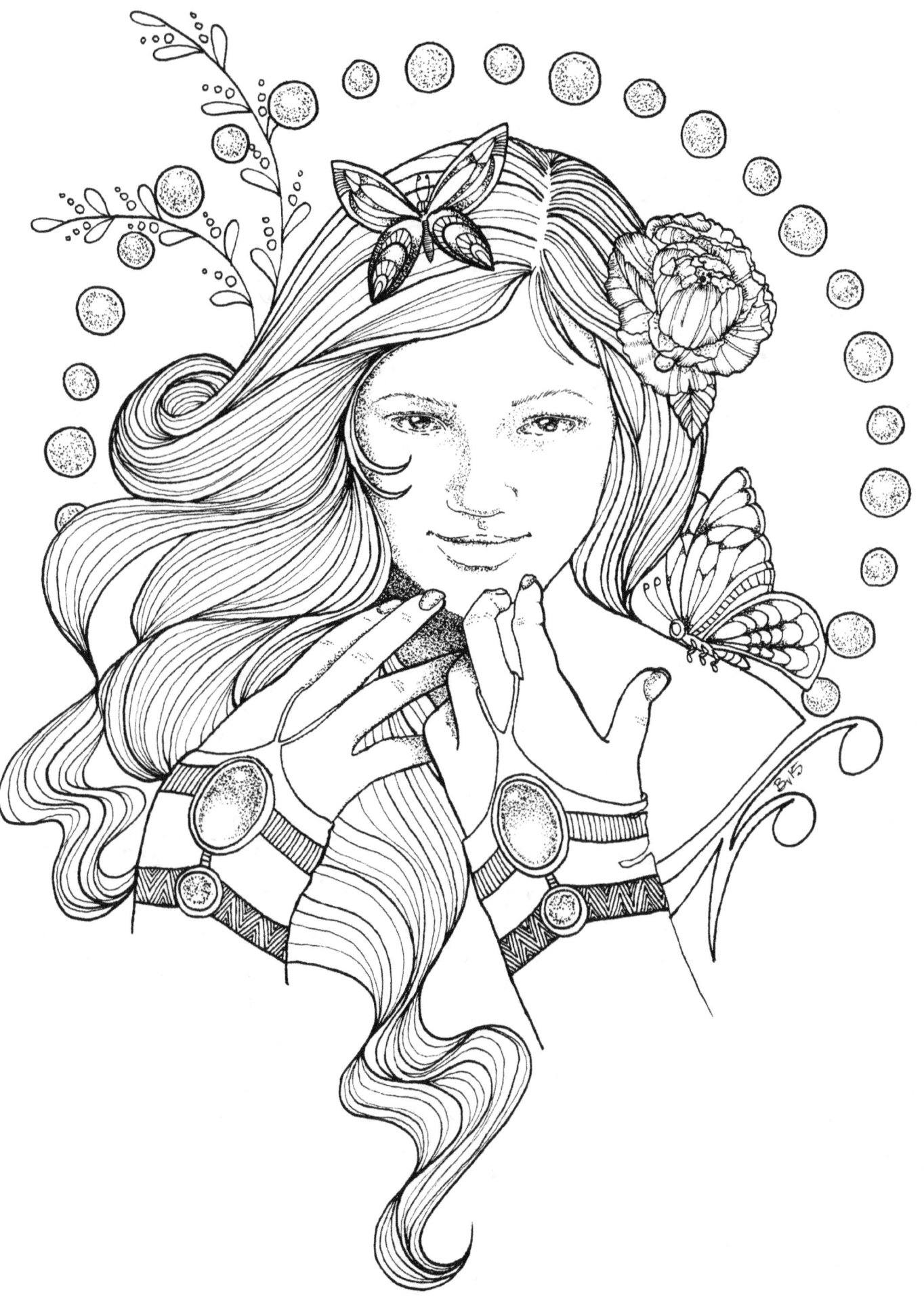

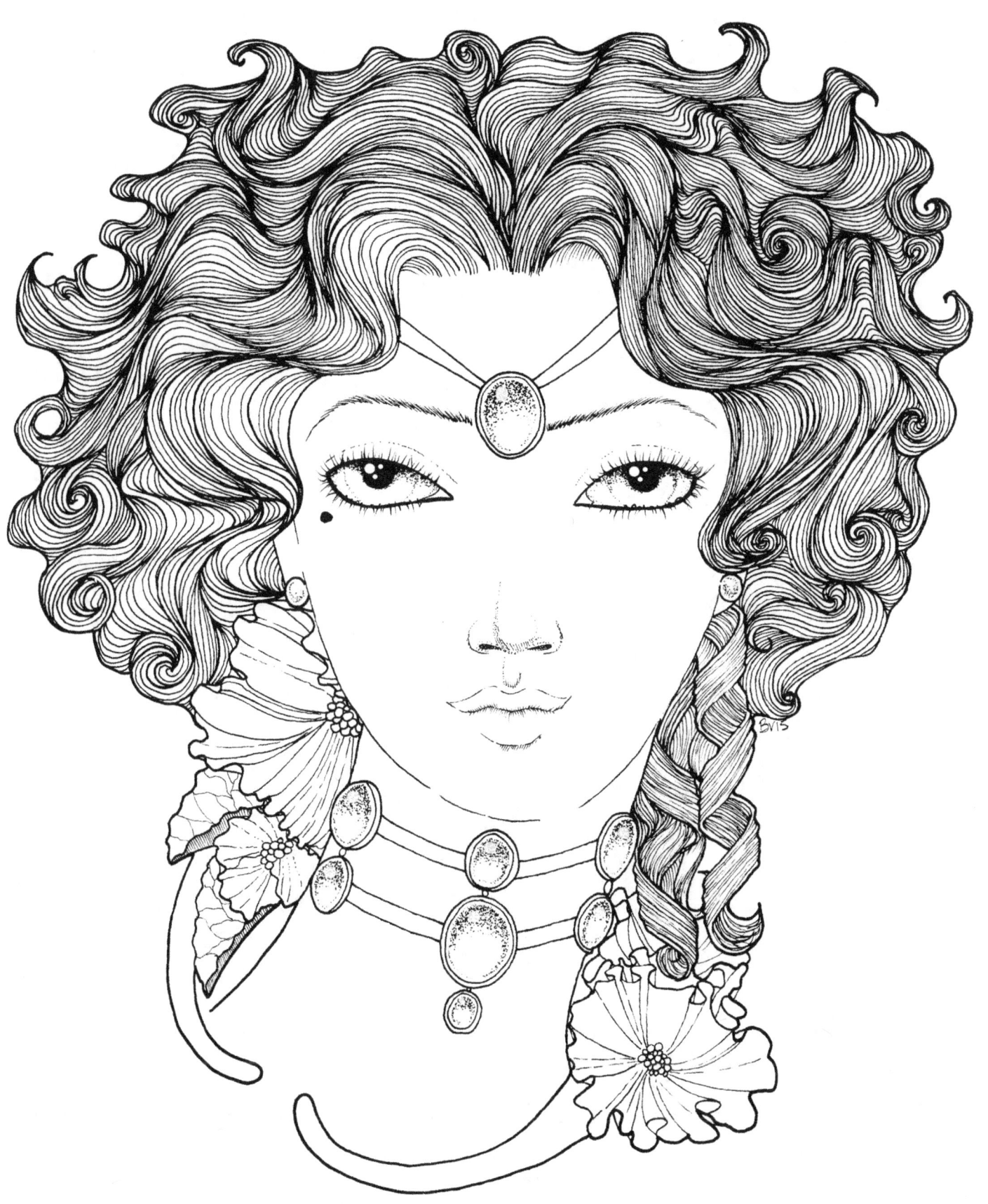

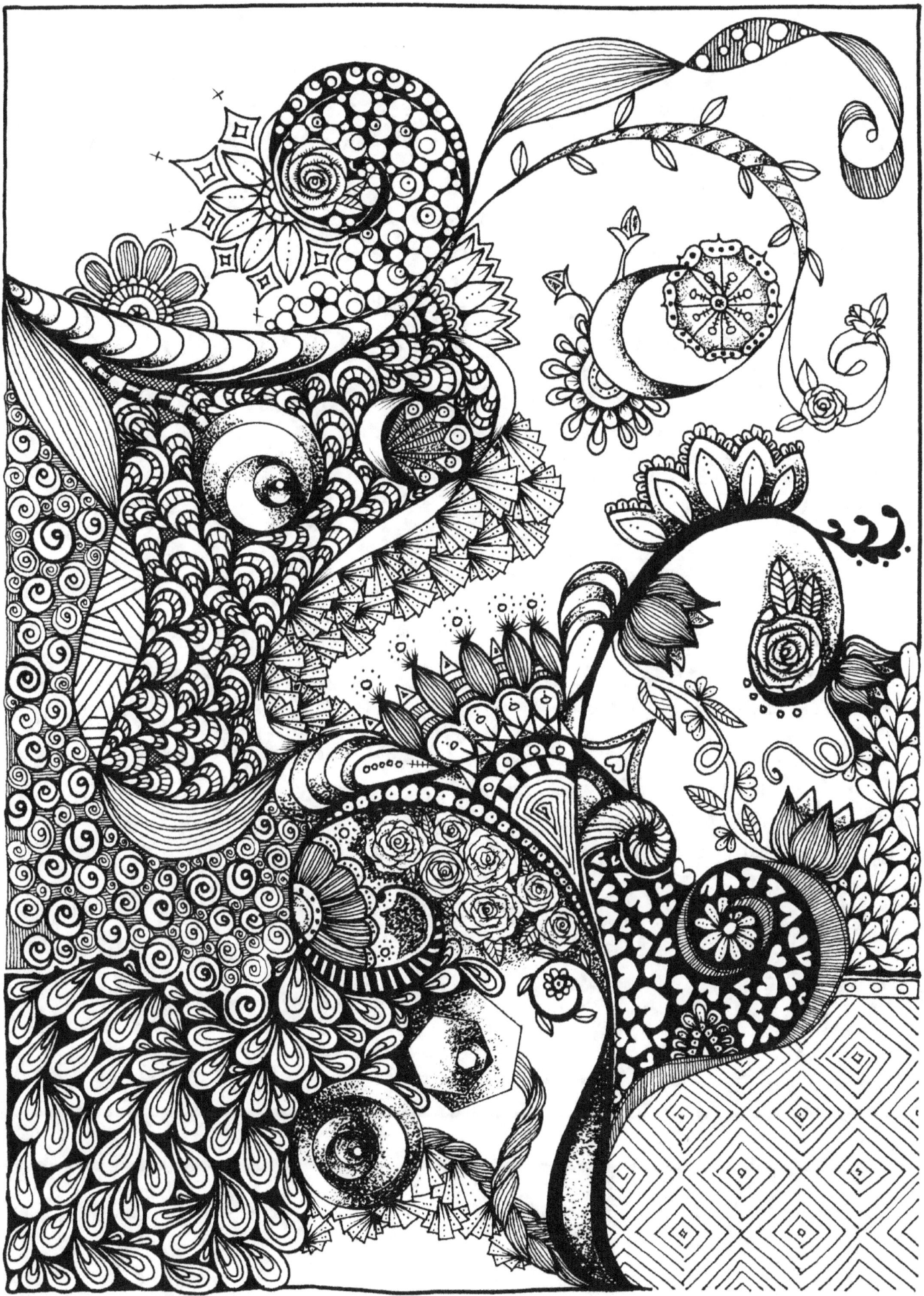

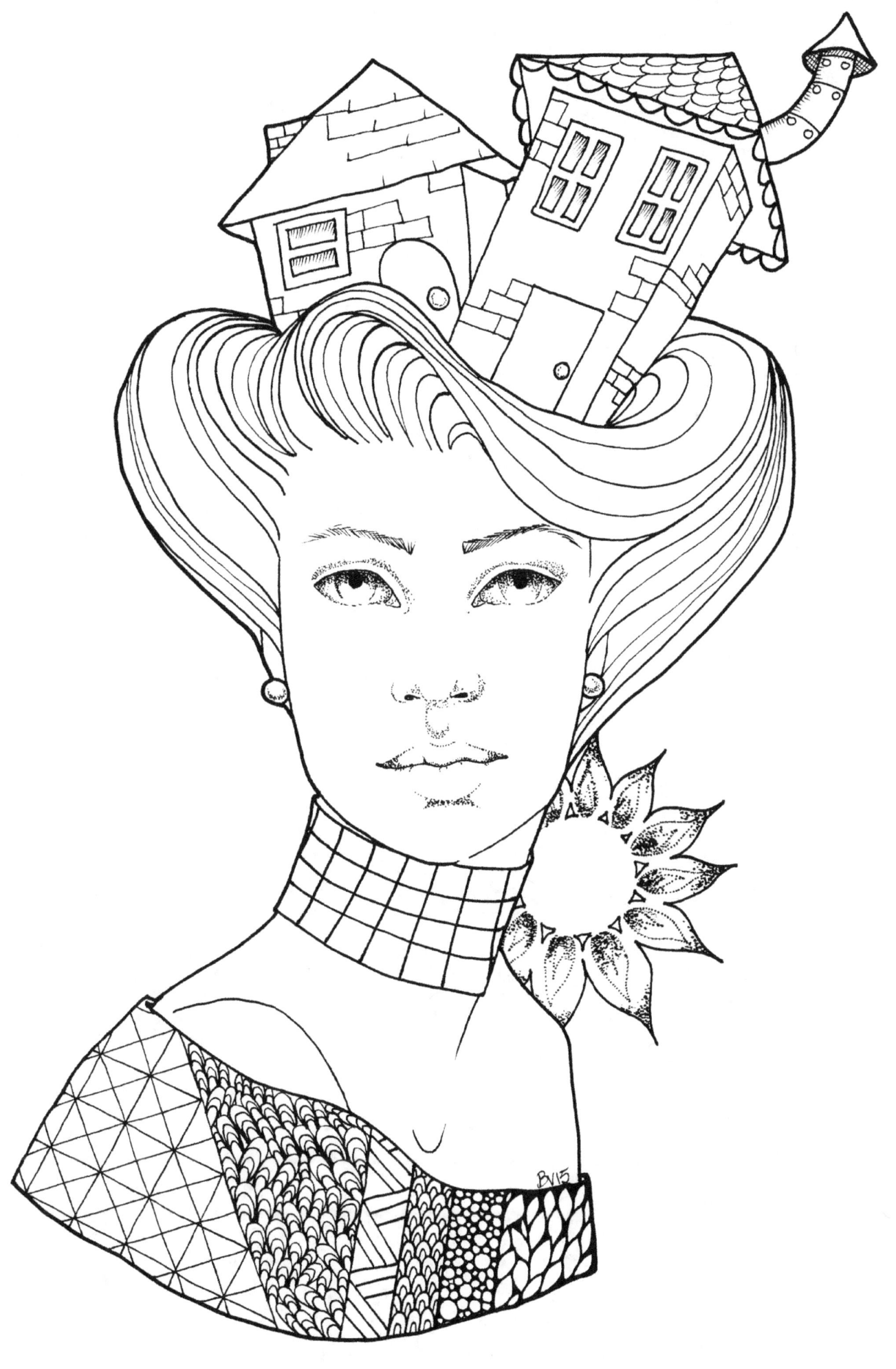

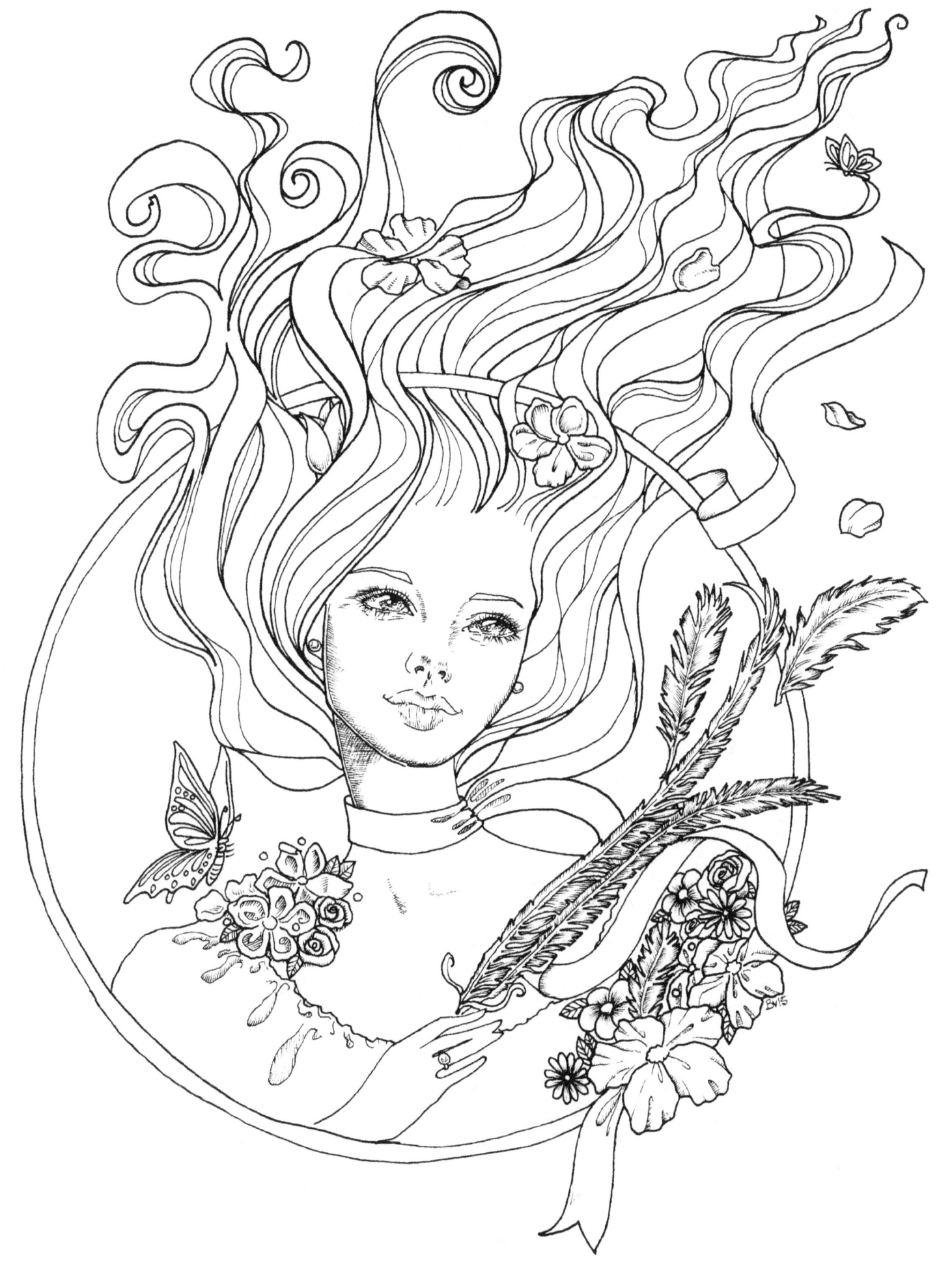

Contact Info

Facebook: www.facebook.com/bevchoyart
Etsy: www.bevchoyart.etsy.com
Email: bevchoy70@gmail.com
Instagram: bevchoy

www.facebook.com/GlobalDoodleGems

My work can also be found in

Colors of Whimsy
Colors of Whimsy II
GDG Volume I
GDG MiniBook I
GDG MiniBook 2
GDG Special Flowers Edition

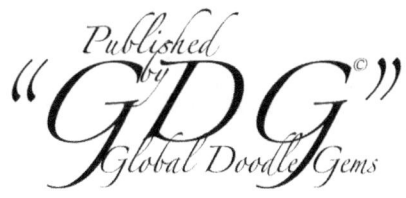